Whiteout

Whiteout

My Racism—Brief Anecdotal Snapshots

Lyn G. Brakeman

RESOURCE *Publications* • Eugene, Oregon

WHITEOUT
My Racism—Brief Anecdotal Snapshots

Copyright © 2025 Lyn G. Brakeman. All rights reserved. Except for brief quotations in critical publications or reviews, no part of this book may be reproduced in any manner without prior written permission from the publisher. Write: Permissions, Wipf and Stock Publishers, 199 W. 8th Ave., Suite 3, Eugene, OR 97401.

Resource Publications
An Imprint of Wipf and Stock Publishers
199 W. 8th Ave., Suite 3
Eugene, OR 97401

www.wipfandstock.com

PAPERBACK ISBN: 979-8-3852-4530-7
HARDCOVER ISBN: 979-8-3852-4531-4
EBOOK ISBN: 979-8-3852-4532-1

VERSION NUMBER 07/29/25

I dedicate this book to my four adult children who carried on with their own precious, lives with dignity, creativity, good humor, love, and humility in the midst of my mid-life breakout. Not one of them has ever shown a trace of racist behavior.

I dedicate this book to Richard John Simeone, my second husband and brother priest, who read my writings and occasionally grumbled, "You can't say that!" He is younger by three years, yet we share August 7th as our birthday. My seniority entitles me to say that anyway. We laugh together a lot.

Divine love is a love that clothes us, enfolds us, and embraces us and . . . completely surrounds us, never to leave us.
Julian of Norwich (born 1342)

Contents

Introduction | 1

Act One. In The Beginning... | 4
Scene One. Dinah And Lou   4
Scene Two. Olga   5
Scene Three Fred   5
Scene Four. Puerto Rican Girls   6

Act Two. Falling Apart | 8
Scene Five. Remembering Hurts   8
Scene Six. Carol Lee   9
Scene Seven. Snowy White Colorlessness   10
Scene Eight. Dr.Mc   12

Act Three. Almighty Insanity | 13
Scene Nine. The Bible   13
Scene Ten. Betty Singer/*Ave Maria (With Color Diagram)*   14

Act Four. Homogeneity—At What Cost? | 16
Scene Eleven. On The School Bus & Hazards Thereof   16
Scene Twelve Gunnar Myrdal   18

CONTENTS

Act Five. High School Blizzard. Race-Blind | 20
Scene Thirteen. First Kiss   20
Scene Fourteen. The Right White Boy Named Bill   21

Act Six. Wounds Of Privilege. College And More. | 23
Scene Fifteen. Wealth   23
Scene Sixteen. Social Disorganization. My Rights?   25
Scene Seventeen. The Chaplain   27
Scene Eighteen. A Psych. Test   28

Act Seven. Spain | 30
Scene Nineteen. Job—The Guy and the Vision   31
Scene Twenty. Que Hay?   32

Act Eight. Independence? Racism-S | 35
Scene Twenty-One. Love *and* Marriage?   35
Scene Twenty-Two. Love *and* Awakening. The Sixties. Daughters, Namesake Son and Heir *And* Moving South   37
Scene Twenty-Three. Salvation?   38

Act Nine. The Seventies | 41
Scene Twenty-Four. New Baby. New Rector. New Sorrow.   41
Scene Twenty-Five. *Dominus Flevit. (Small Picture of Teardrop Church, Israel)*   42
Scene Twenty-Six. Spacious Hearts. Love *and* Divorce? Hope?   43

Act Ten. In The Dark With Glimmers in Grief | 45
Scene Twenty-Seven. Ether   45
Scene Twenty-Eight. The Relational Way, A New Psychology.   46

Scene Twenty-Nine. The Rev. Richard (Dick) John Simeone. *And* Remembering Theologians (John Macquarrie, Søren Kierkegaard)   47
Scene Thirty. What About Sex-Ism?   49

Act Eleven. Emergence Into The Light. Coming Alive! | 51
Scene Thirty-One. Word And Sacrament   51
Scene Thirty-Two. What About Biblical Characters?   53

Act Twelve. Rights And Duties Revisited | 55
Scene Thirty-Three. My Jesuit   55
Scene Thirty-Four. My Rights?   57
Scene Thirty-Five. What About Church Rights?   58
Scene Thirty-Six. The Perfect Paying Job?   60

Act Thirteen. Ongoing Formation | 62
Scene Thirty-Seven. All-From-Above Exclusively?   62
Scene Thirty-Eight. Sower Parable Revisited. Ready. Set Go?   64

Act Fourteen. Leapings | 65
Scene Thirty-Nine. Powering Up   65
Scene Forty. Choices Of Pain And Gain   66

Act Fifteen. Words Coming Alive | 69
Scene Forty-One. Potentiation. The First Day   69
Scene Forty-Two. Inerrancy? (Photo Of Jim Echols, In Color.)   71
Scene Forty-Three. Immanence   74

Act Sixteen. New Testament | 75
Scene Forty-Four. Luke Timothy Johnson, Immanence   75
Scene Forty-Five. Bill Muehl, Preaching (Small B/W Photo)   81

CONTENTS

Act Seventeen. Practicing Immanence | 81
Scene Forty-Six. Such A Deal!   83
Scene Forty-Seven. Wedding.   84

Act Eighteen. Learning Without Studying. | 85
Scene Forty-Eight. EFM   85
Scene Forty-Nine. Lessons On Dying From The Dying   86
Scene Fifty. Lessons From Blacks On Being Black   88
Scene Fifty-One. Lessons From Alkies On Sobriety   89

Act Nineteen. How Holy Is Holy? | 92
Scene Fifty-Two. Sex Holy?   92
Scene Fifty-Three. Anger Holy?   94
Scene Fifty-Four. Money Holy? Ordained So.   94

Act Twenty. Ongoing/Remembered Formation | 97
Scene Fifty-Five. Spiritual Directions.   97
Scene Fifty-Six. Madeleine L'Engle   98

Act Twenty-One. Independence For Whom? | 100
Scene Fifty-Seven. Reading Rita.   100
Scene Fifty-Eight. Toni   101

Act Twenty-Two. Embodiments | 103
Scene Fifty-Nine. Infamy Ongoing. Holy. Liberating.   106
Scene Sixty. Passive Aggression Laid Bare.   109
Scene Sixty-One. Earrings. Altar Guild. Marine.   110

Act Twenty-Three. Saints/Sinners? | 111
Scene Sixty-Two. Mary Virgin/Mother/Theotokos   111
Scene Sixty-Three. My Grandmothers.   113
Scene Sixty-Four. My First Patient/Addiction Rehab.   114

CONTENTS

Act Twenty-Four. Trustworthy Spirituality | 117
Scene Sixty-Five. Prayers In The Bible   117
Scene Sixty-Six. A Prayer Rose.   118
Scene Sixty-Seven. Breaking Up The Old Boys' Club   119
Scene Sixty-Eight. The Syrophoenician (Canaanite) Woman   119
Scene Sixty-Nine. Deeper Pain. Deeper Prayer.   120

Act Twenty Five. Moving | 122
Scene Seventy. Gloucester-Ism?   122
Scene Seventy-One. Back To A City   125
Scene Seventy-Two. Writing My Memoir   127

Act Twenty-Six. Healing Mentors Along My Way | 129

Act Twenty-Seven. Seasoning *All* Saints | 132
Scene Seventy-Three. Finding Particular Places   132
Scene Seventy-Four. Deepening Racial Potentiation   133
Scene Seventy-Five. Blessing All Saints   135

Act Twenty-Eight. Holiness Of Word/Sacrament Whose? | 137
Scene Seventy-Six. Scriptures   137
Scene Seventy-Seven. Every Story Needs A Ritual
(Photo B/W, Heschel)   138
Scene Seventy-Eight. Daily Life Sacramentality.   139
Scene Seventy-Nine. Learning To Read The Flesh   141

Act Twenty-Nine. Retirement? | 144
Scene Eighty. Keeping On Keeping On   144
Scene Eighty-One. Topography?   145
Scene Eighty-Two. Caged Birds?   146
Scene Eighty-Three. "We Flesh. . ."   147

CONTENTS

Scene Eighty-Four. Recitatif   149
Scene Eighty-Five. Personal Emotional Intelligence   151

Act Thirty. Living It All Together? | 153
Scene Eighty-Six. The Rev. Dr. Pauli Murray   154
Scene Eighty-Seven. Quirky History, A Mural, And A Coin (Colored Photo Of Mural At Yale)   156

Act Thirty-One. Ideally Retired In Whitesville | 159
Scene Eighty-Eight. Senior Packing It In Together   159

Epilogue | 162
    Divinity   162
    The Late Rt. Rev. Barbara C. Harris   162
    The Late Madeleine L'Engle   163
    Family/Friends/Proofer   163

INTRODUCTION

I grew up with God practically as my personal possession, thanks to my earliest spiritual experience chatting with a silent listening God I'd first met in a book called "The Little Book About God" by Lauren Ford. I sat crosslegged under a large cloth-covered dining table and babbled all my woes and all my wanderings to God. Thus I first assumed that many things in the world that look silly or obviously harmful or tragic may, nonetheless, be godsends.

* * *

As I write now I am in my eighties. I still tune into divine whisperings or guffaws. One morning out of the wild blue yonder of my prayer-dreams I looked out the window and saw many brightly colored leaves crisp up and flutter to their death. I closed my eyes quickly against the death of the leaves, against my fears—just against.

A word arrived on my mental screen. *Whiteout.*

Whiteout?

Fully awake by now, I re-bonded with my computer and its dark black screen in front of the white key board, I wrote that word—*Whiteout.* What? A whiteout is a blizzard, a driving white snow—*blinding*. It's just like a blackout, which is an eclipse from light/ sunlight—*blinding*. There's no difference between a blackout and a whiteout.

I lived my whole life among white people like me. Had I been blinded all my life? Was I toxically whiteIST, exclusively valuing people with white skin? No. That would completely betray my spiritual experience of a God who created everything and always loved every bit of it—enough to endow it all with freedom. Damned dumb idea, in my opinion, yet the only idea with enough breadth and depth to thrive.

Ringing in my mind was a statement I'd heard at a writers' conference in the 1990s. Black poet, Ralph Ellison (1913–1994) said: "If you don't talk about racism, you erase us." So if I didn't talk about racism I could erase whites also? I laughed at the enormity of this topic.

It's amusing to consider the product called Wite-Out. When you brush its white thickness over your black typo, the black immediately reappears right through it. It doesn't work, this phony product.

No coverups ever work, do they?

I knew I would have to write *Whiteout* from within my personal experience, not from an academic or abstract perspective. I would explore "racismS" from inside out. I would write *reflectively*, giving this difficult topic my full attention, integrating all positive and negative experiences into a whole system of thoughts, feelings, and insights. Thus I'd try to avoid being *refllexive*, knee-jerking my way along according to traditional cultural norms and/or how others think I *should* think or feel.

God, the one I'd first met under the table, gave me a conscience and expected me to know that there is nothing *supreme* about any

INTRODUCTION

race or skin color as long as one doesn't get blinded by singularity, or add -ISM to suggest the supreme superiority of one perspective, one race, one sex, one religion, one polity.

This is the bit-by-bit story of how I've learned to be white without succumbing to *whiteout*.

ACT ONE. IN THE BEGINNING.

I met God when I was a young child. At the same time I met myself—wordy, thoughtful and inquisitive. I learned that I mattered—no matter what.

I was born in 1938, into a huge city called New York on a tiny island called Manhattan, in the middle of a river called Hudson or East, on an avenue called Lexington, in a building numbered 1435. Everything was safe and happy there. My favorite place to play was in the basement where I met my first best friends.

SCENE ONE. DINAH AND LOU

Dinah was our laundress. Her teenage daughter Lou babysat for me. I spent time with them in the basement where the Laundry was. Lou and I raced around playing hide and seek while Dinah scrubbed the clothes and ironed them all—our clothes not hers. I loved Dinah and Lou and easily assumed that they were family. I worried that they lived in the basement, which was concrete and ugly and full of cells with locks where people stored their old suitcases and other junk. My mother reassured me that Dinah and Lou had their own home on 125th Street—31 whole blocks away from where I lived. When Lou babysat she took the subway

ACT ONE. IN THE BEGINNING.

home. Once my mother gave her fare. I never wondered about the color of Dinah's and Lou's skin. However, I never understood why I couldn't go play at their house.

I was learning how to behave white.

SCENE TWO. OLGA

Olga was a new student in my private girls school called Nightingale Bamford, in New York City. We girls wore ugly blue uniforms, but we also learned to speak French and a little Latin. Olga came in fourth grade. She was Russian. There was something a little "wrong" about being Russian, and about Olga's accent. Such identifiers made her prey. She was different. Some of us fourth grade girls used to chase her down a few city blocks and taunt her. She was a fast runner. I was a bully, learning about shame and shaming, hallmarks of fear-based racism and other prejudices.

SCENE THREE. FRED

My dad, the fourth of six children, grew up in the early 1900's in Morristown New Jersey, an affluent suburb of Manhattan. He and one older brother were the only two who, as adults, moved "away from home"—all the way into the big city. As a child, I didn't know the word *heresy*. Nevertheless, such moving away was like family heresy, according to the Gillespie family's code of expectations: no one moved out of Morristown.

Every Sunday there was, what I learned to call a command performance—THE family Sunday dinner. We gathered around the big table. The dinner was served by Fred. He held each course before us for assent, and then he served the food onto our plates. I got the idea that one did not refuse any of these courses, even if a food choice was something quite unacceptable, such as, in my opinion, seedy squash.

After dinner Ma, a would-be opera singer and the family matriarch, would gather "her boys," my Dad among them, around the piano for singing. They all had wonderful deep voices. That's when I got bored and snuck into the kitchen to talk with Fred. Fred was a funny, kind, and handsome black man who, when Ma stomped her foot onto a hidden button under the table, would appear like magic. "More potatoes, Fred," she'd say, and Fred would return to the kitchen and bring forth potatoes. Fred was like a waiter in a restaurant, but he lived somewhere in the house. I asked where? In "the servant quarters" I was told. I wanted to visit Fred, but the "servants' quarters" were off limits. Why? I was getting the idea that Fred, like Dinah and Lou, was somehow separate. I didn't yet associate that separateness with skin color, probably because the family's other "servant," Nettie, was white. She too lived in "the servants' quarters"—also off limits. I was learning about separation for no good reason.

By the time I reached twelve, I was perched on the cusp of hormonal torrents, and lived with the dim memory of a childhood wound that left me intensely aware of cruelty to other people who were defenseless and tormented for no reason—no reason at all.

SCENE FOUR. PUERTO RICAN GIRLS

I was old enough, eleven and three quarters, to walk with a friend to the RKO movie theater at 86th Street on Lexington Avenue just eight blocks from where I lived. I will never forget this mighty and grand theater, nor how mighty and grand I felt going to the movies with a friend, and no parent.

Once while walking home from the movies, my friend and I were accosted by a group of Puerto Rican girls. They yelled, screamed, grabbed our scarves, and pulled our hair. I was terrified. We broke free. I ran faster than I thought I could. I'd overheard my parents talking about all those Puerto Ricans who could take over our neighborhood. *My* neighborhood? I feared them, because this

ACT ONE. IN THE BEGINNING.

was *my* city, *my* home. I told my mother about my fear. Maybe if I hadn't told her we might have stayed in the city. I might have avoided "white flight," which meant moving out of my city to the suburbs. All because of our white skin.

I secretly fumed and raged and grieved about this radical displacement. Later I identified this "white flight" as "white fright." It felt like that Bible story called The Exodus—all about Moses leading Jews out of Egypt. I'd heard it in Sunday School. Why did God make them move? To escape slavery. Was this like Fred being exiled to live in another place for servants only? But Fred wasn't Jewish was he? Was I? I wasn't Puerto Rican either, but I soon would get "exodused" anyway. Fear kept me silent.

ACT TWO. FALLING APART.

Learnings dictate rules, practices, avoidances, and denials, unspoken yet obvious to everyone—except to me, a budding nonconformist naif. To be displaced while perched on the lip edge of hormonal torrents was traumatic. My parents who'd moved us to the suburbs called it suburban salvation. I called it becoming a maturing adolescent, which was a pile-up of mysterious horrors, including the loss of my best friends.

SCENE FIVE. REMEMBERING HURTS

In the grand city theater, Radio City Music Hall, when I was eight, I had been sexually molested by an old man with a long white beard, not like Santa Claus's, but scraggly, more like God's as pictured in books. The old man sat to my left and ran his withered hand up my left leg. Over and over, further up into my underpants, his hand explored. I felt an insidiously creeping combination of pain and pleasure all at once. I was paralyzed, except for my left hand that kept removing his right hand. His beard, like his skin, was white just like God's in my book. Was God white?

As a child, I'd unknowingly been opened to the wounds of whiteness, femaleness, sexuality, age, abuse, and shame. I could not "white" anything out. I was learning about the dynamics of

ACT TWO. FALLING APART.

sadism, predator and prey, the painful power of secrecy, and the innocence of a child.

My mind imprisoned my secret for many years. When I finally told my mother she shrugged and said: "Such things happen, darling."

I was beginning to wonder if it was toxic to be white, or was it just my gender—or both?

SCENE SIX. CAROL LEE

Carol Lee became my best friend in Westhampton, Long Island, where we city folk summered to get away from the overheated metropolis. Friends make everything better. So do two-wheeler bikes. Our family had been spending summers at a farm in upstate New York, where I had my own pony and a best friend, but my parents, I'm assuming, were social climbing, so we switched to THE Hamptons—another move for which I would resent them. I'd become an expert at listening in, a form of espionage through which I picked up all kinds of scraps and nuances about class and race. I felt like a teenage Nancy Drew, puzzling over many mysteries I didn't understand.

Soon I became afraid of being a snob. I'd heard my mother and her friends talk with disdain about "snobs" on Park Avenue. We'd lived on Lexington Avenue and were therefore not snobs, I figured. I also happily claimed that we were *not* snobs, because we were in WESThampton, not EASThampton. Could geography itself breed a kind of racism?

I also didn't think of my parents as rich, mostly because my father always, always worried about money. He worked in advertising on Madison Avenue. He advertised soup while my mother advertised me and bought me clothes galore. Sometimes I overheard their arguments about my mother's extravagance and felt guilty about my clothes—not guilty enough, however, to dissuade my mother from such excesses. Still, I figured my parents must have been somewhat rich, because even in Westhampton they joined a private beach club.

* * * *

I fell in love with the ocean—its waves, its vastness. No one could be excluded from the ocean, right? And no one owned it. In August I would turn twelve, an edgy age, especially when you look about ten. Did I want my party at the beach club or at home? I chose the beach club, and excitedly told Carol Lee all about it.

The beach club was exclusively for white people. Carol Lee was black. I did not understand. The ocean didn't care. I told my parents they should tell their club to make an exception. They didn't. Nor did they tell me what to do. I was furious. I had to choose between Carol Lee and the damn beach club. For the first time, or the most conscious time, my life choices became *my* ethics, *my* racism. I chose the beach club and demanded another party for me and Carol Lee. I went to two parties, but I hurt my best friend. I hurt myself, too. I do remember that I did *not* tell Carol Lee about the beach club's rules.

Who did I think I was protecting? I smoldered with inner pain. Carol Lee wasn't a "servant." Nor could I blame Russia as I had with Olga. Neither could I blame the metropolis for the Puerto Rican influx. This was me. I had made a racist choice. I suddenly *experienced* racism in my flesh. It hurt.

SCENE SEVEN. SNOWY WHITE COLORLESSNESSS

White is a non-color. It felt like Minute Rice—all white, all-instant, all-easy, just like the suburban town my parents chose to move to, Darien, Connecticut. There were private beach clubs nearby, all of them segregated, all of them on Long Island sound. My parents joined the private one. I went to the public beach! At least the

ACT TWO. FALLING APART.

school was public with boys in it, yet pretty much all white. So I puzzled about color lines, grieved, and prayed for boobs.

I missed the city—its colorfulness, its buzz. I didn't know the word "diversity" then, but I *felt* the absence of color. Colorlessness felt safe *and* squirmy—white-on-white bland,

Finding a new best friend helped me feel safe. Her name was Annie. Her skin was whiter than mine, and she had white blonde hair to match. Most importantly, she actually understood the "facts of life"—sex. We bonded immediately. We both were smart and made The National Honor Society (NHS). The custom was that a student who was already an NHS member introduced an inductee. Annie introduced me.

School helped my self-esteem. I was smart. I loved A's. They paved my way to self-esteem. I was also learning to run things with my mind—majoring in thinking. As to emotions, they were hidden though painful, because now in my new public school I did not fit in physically. I needed boobs, maybe a waistline—a little stature. I needed to menstruate—right away if possible. Annie said it would come.

What is the most "rational" thing a girl of thirteen—failed immigrant to suburbia, missing her first best friend Carol Lee, entering junior high school, lost in a sea of boys and boobs, and slow to mature—can do? Find the right book.

I dug out my first "right" book, *The Little Book About God* by Lauren Ford, published in 1934. This time it was different. Yes, God still listened to "weeny" sounds, but when I re-read it I was arrested by the scene in which the girl was all alone, weeping, at a kitchen table, because there was war. An angel finally showed up. I sobbed about my deficient body—an adolescent failure. I needed an angel. My mother showed up.

After warning me never to become a "slut" she hauled me off to a medical doctor for a consultation, myself as the specimen.

SCENE EIGHT. Dr. Mc............

Before I knew enough to protest, this kindly old doctor, coaxed me, with saccharine affect, onto an examination table, spread my legs and lifted my feet into stirrups—not like the stirrups on a saddle, although I was in for a ride.

"Let's just take a little peek, shall we?" the doctor said. Who *we*? A peek at *what*? I quickly realized that *we* were not going to check for my appendix, and that *I* couldn't possibly "take a peek" at my genitals from this position. I froze. From inside my personal frozen whiteout, I overheard the old doctor say to my mother: "She may have difficulty conceiving a child. Small cervix. . ."

"Thank God!" My mother exclaimed as we drove home and she chattered. I stayed sullen and silent. Even I didn't realize what a cauldron of contempt I was developing—for myself, my own body, the predatory old doctor whom I secretly called Dr. McAsshole, because his name started with *Mc*, and for my mother who thanked God I wasn't a slut.

For *God's* sake I shouldn't be a slut? For *God's* sake I shouldn't get pregnant?

ACT THREE. ALMIGHTY INSANITY.

Guess what? God got a maiden named Mary pregnant! This spared her from slutdom, cervical anxiety, or sexism; hence, religion could immediately call her "holy" and give her a special set of prayers. For what?

To get us females pregnant, or to keep us from getting pregnant?

SCENE NINE. THE BIBLE

At fourteen, I needed God to talk.

In church they called the Holy Bible God's Word. What could be better? I compulsively read the whole huge book, skipping most of Leviticus. What I learned was not exactly the personal affirmation I expected. I learned that God's world was called Creation. From the beginning everyone messed up, and yet somehow everyone fit in. Like a huge jigsaw puzzle there was a place for everyone and everything. Seriously, it was astounding.

There were rules or course—straight-out commandments about what NOT to do. The people did it all, so God sent them pissed off prophets, crazy with rage and giving the best persuasive political speeches I'd ever heard. This God was seriously the dumbest parent I'd ever heard of. Every single time God and the people broke up they got back together—every single time. Incredible!

Jesus, star of the New Testament, whom everyone thought was God about whom I wondered, was as furious about such messes as God was. He was Jewish and taught right behavior, even embraced demons and miscreants. Jesus's travel plan, "Let's go to Jerusalem" was so dumb I cringed.

I warmed to the stories for their own sake. Women like Mary Magdalene, possibly a slutty type herself, became Jesus's best friend. Old Sarah laughed at God's assurance that she'd get pregnant. At her age? How profoundly, divinely anti-biological. I laughed. There was even a young shepherd boy named David, God's chosen one who sinned so big he almost got killed by a raging giant. Sarah, by then even older than my grandmother, became pregnant. There was also a black slave in there who was set free according to divine orders. And young Mary, a virgin of Nazareth did get pregnant and gave birth to Jesus out of wedlock, but God gave her a rationale: tell them the angel named Gabriel did it.

This Bible was crazy, ridiculously hopeful, paradoxical—roomy enough for me AND Carol Lee. This was called GRACE, but I don't think churches knew much about it.

SCENE TEN. BETTY SINGER

Betty Singer had a singing voice unlike any I'd heard.

ACT THREE. ALMIGHTY INSANITY.

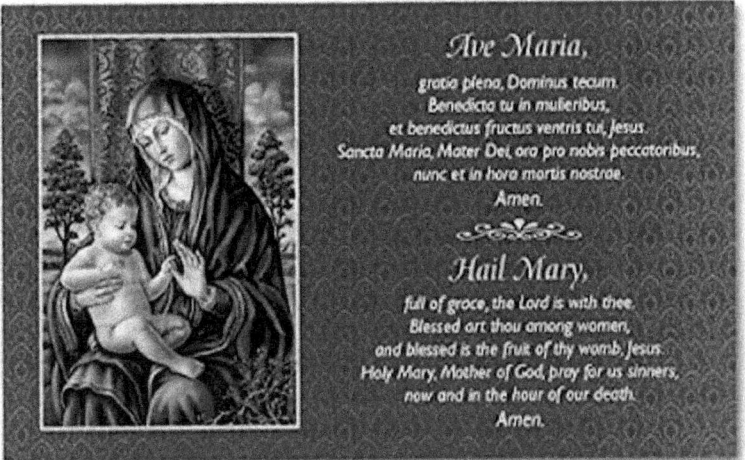

We junior high school girls circled around her at recess and begged her—beseeched her to sing *Ave Maria*. We swooned. I didn't understand a word. It was in Latin, but it sure didn't make my Latin teacher's reading list. Betty told us this song was Catholic. It was in the Bible, she thought. When Betty sang my mind stopped all its worrying.

The seeds were planted for my later investigatory explorations of those Catholics. For now, I had to get on with my own biology, and make sure God didn't get *me* pregnant.

ACT FOUR. HOMOGENEITY —AT WHAT COST?

My mother said Catholics weren't really American, and yet we were Americans. Who could be American? Was Carol Lee? Was America for whites only? We waved flags and cheered for this American dream. But was this dream really true for *every* American, even blacks, or Catholics, or confused adolescents like me? *White-on-white* cruelty reigned as far my eye could see.

SCENE ELEVEN. ON THE SCHOOL BUS & THE HAZARDS THEREOF

There is probably no culture more cruel, life-threatening, and traumatizing than that of a junior high school bus—that long orange monster that rolled around town and picked up strays who gathered at a designated SCHOOL BUS STOP.

Unless you were *totally* normal you were a target for torturous humor. For girls, normal meant cute, perky, flirty, in a cashmere sweater with obvious upper body endowments and a wasp waist, ripe for "slutdom." For boys, normal meant swaggering and strutting and punching, panting after "sluts" as if they had something no one else did, and/or boys had something indispensable in itself.

ACT FOUR. HOMOGENEITY—AT WHAT COST?

On the bus, I shifted from side to side in my seat, pulling at my skirt while trying to puff up my hair without upsetting the overweight pile of books shoulder-strapped and poised on one hip. I sat in the front of the bus—normal. The boys sat in the back, awaiting their prey.

A boy named Percival flunked the "normalcy" profile—catastrophically. He didn't strut, he lumbered. He played the violin which he carried with him onto the bus. He wore thick glasses. He was borderline obese. Every day when he thudded onto the bus the boys cooed and wooed him to the back of the bus where they'd gathered for the massacre. They forced their victim down onto the floor. They took his violin, removed it from its case and played it till it squeaked in protest; they called him names; they spit on him, and removed his glasses; they held him down so he could not get off at his stop. Every day, he had to walk home. And, to his eternal junior high shame, he cried.

I will never forget this boy. I felt nauseated. I cried. I prayed. I said nothing. I was a coward. Years later I tried to look him up on Google, which despite its near-divine status, failed to find him. Please God, let him wear contact lenses, and be a brilliant violinist in some symphony orchestra.

There was a female version of this horror show. She was overweight, too, but had a "normal" name—until she received the nickname "Hairy Legs." Girls are just as mean as boys but less physical. We relentlessly teased her, because her unshaved legs were, well, totally abnormal. She said that her mother wouldn't let her shave her legs, and back then girls only wore skirts. I cursed her stupid mother.

The school bus driver, Mr. Fitz, was the owner of the school bus franchise. He was so fat there was no space between the lower edge of the steering wheel and his paunch. I glared at him to see if I could somehow get him to stop the cruelty. He did nothing. I saw him smirking.

I felt tortured myself. My way of managing my horror was to demand that my mother drive me to school. I was getting good at lobbying, which meant wearing my poor mother down. I would never ride the bus again.

* * *

These school bus victims suffered for things they could do nothing about. This made me wonder if bullying behavior was racist? Was it white-on-white bullying? It was the 1950s. I knew that some people lived "on the other side of the tracks"—not as good as our side, I was told. I guessed it was something like the different sides of New York City—east and west with Central Park in the middle.

My best friend Annie lived on that "other side of the tracks." My mother sometimes complained about having to drive us back and forth, but having Annie as a best friend saved my life. We both felt a little left out, so one day we pricked our fingers till some blood came out. Then we touched them and called it our blood covenant, another word I'd seen in the Bible.

Everyone in my school in Darien, Connecticut was white, or maybe Italian. Bullying was a form of teenage racism— toxic for all of us. I wished I could talk with Carol Lee about all this.

SCENE TWELVE. GUNNER MYRDAL

Throughout junior and senior high schools there was a required course called Problems of Democracy. Some schools called it Civics. It was education to help students understand how our government worked—or didn't. Our teacher was Mr. Beckwith. I liked him, and I liked the course. I don't remember what texts we read, but I do remember that Mr. Beckwith talked, in just about

ACT FOUR. HOMOGENEITY—AT WHAT COST?

every class, about this ONE book by Gunnar Myrdal. It was about racism. Why was he mentioning that when we all were white, and Myrdal's book was *not* assigned reading for the class? Were whites even a race?

Not until I was writing this book did I look him up.

Gunnar Myrdal (1898-1987) was a sociologist, an economist, and a Swedish Nobel laureate, also a professor at Stockholm University in Sweden. According to record, Myrdal was openly anti-Nazi. His major work was *An American Dilemma. The Negro Problem and Modern Democracy*, published in 1944, a time of war, fought for the sake of something called Peace—peaceful coexistence. Myrdal advocated for the welfare of the world, and even wrote an article about removing "the beam in our eyes" from the biblical saying of Jesus, according to the New Testament gospel of Matthew 7:1-5. This "beam" referred to the hypocrisy of passing judgment on another's blindness without taking stock of one's own blindness. Both whiteout and blackout are race-blind!

* * * *

Back in the 1950s, I was learning that even a curriculum could be racist. People behind closed doors decided what texts students could read. Taxes funded public education. Our teacher was trying to let us know what we were not supposed to know: money controls what is taught, and maybe white people *should* pay higher taxes?

Who did our American dream *really* include?

The Bible again seemed to be the right book for me, because I did not think this huge God who apparently created the whole darned Earth could be racist. I wondered.

First, I'd get a boyfriend, handsome if possible.

ACT FIVE. HIGH SCHOOL BLIZZARD?

I was learning to live-race-blind. Is that racist?

Darien High School was full of racial-like categories—jocks, prom queen/cheerleaders, spicks, hoods, wops, nerds, whores, aka sluts, and madonnas like the one named Blessed Mary in Betty Singer's song. As to religious classifications, there were Catholics and everybody else. There were no Jews thanks to an unspoken pernicious agreement among "gentlemen" realtors not to show properties to Jews in some Connecticut shore towns of lower Fairfield County. I lived in one of those towns. I had to fit in.

In truth, however, there wasn't much social mobility at all in high school. Fitting in had to do with appearances. Luckily I wasn't overweight or slat-thin. I had a pencil skirt and a cashmere sweater. I could stuff a little Kleenex into my bra until I grew the requisite breasts and found a steady boyfriend who met requirements—mine and those of the silent caste system I apparently was in.

SCENE THIRTEEN. FIRST KISS

Bob was my very first crush. That's what they called it when you felt mentally and emotionally crushed by some combination of

ACT FIVE. HIGH SCHOOL BLIZZARD?

anxiety and hormonal desire—enough to make you inarticulate and lonely. Bob was pathologically shy, so he was easy to flirt with. We went for a twilight walk in the local bird sanctuary. Trees hung over the paths we walked, the air smelled like peaches, and every bird was singing an aria. I felt faint with sheer joy as Bob pulled me close—and closer. His breath smelled.

I needed a date for my sweet sixteen birthday party rolled around at the beach club. *Bob was Catholic.* Would this all-white private beach club allow that? I'd lived this painful scenario before with Carol Lee. Damn! The memory alone made me ache. What else could be outlawed by some -ism or other?

* * * *

I finger-tested the salty waters and dove off the float and into the Long Island sound, my arms parting the cool dark waters like Moses had, or maybe Jesus—down and down as deep as I could without drowning. It helped.

SCENE FOURTEEN. THE RIGHT WHITE BOY NAMED BILL

Bill Brakeman was the most handsome boy I'd ever seen. Even better, he was white and also a failed immigrant like me, transplanted from Chicago as I had been from New York. We first met at one of those teenage parties hosted by the parents of a classmate who was more handicapped than me. I had only imagined myself as fat, the worst thing to be, but this girl was actually fat. There is nothing at all for anyone that's "sweet" about being sixteen.

I lurked at the food table, grazing on celery while longing for a huge piece of chocolate layer cake, when I spotted Bill. He stood in the corner alone with beckoning eyes—not flirting just longing. My heart leaped into his arms. No wonder "Blue Moon" eventually became our song. We saw each other standing there alone with tons of dreams in our hearts and no love of our own. Bill had been going steady with someone else, but she was flirting with another boy. I was a stray. In the game of high school belonging and becoming, steadiness wasn't a strong player, despite cravings thereof.

Bill's and my first official date was the next day. We went to a football game. I didn't understand a thing about football, but that didn't matter, because I was with this boy named Bill who, I was sure, knew what he was doing and drove a chartreuse convertible!

Two teams ran out onto the field; cheerleaders jumped and howled; the announcer blasted: Tarrytown versus North Tarrytown. Not even our school! We laughed and laughed and watched the damn game anyway. That's how I became a couple!

I didn't think of this back then, but Bill was also safe—normal, white, safe.

Something I couldn't then define attacked me. In high school it was called but now recognize as sexual attraction "having the hots." I had them, or my body had them all by itself. Still, my mother aside, I knew you didn't start to date someone just for the "hots." That would be slutty, letting my flesh take the lead!

I was learning about internalized ethnic prejudice—caught in the undertow of the high school caste system whose outer accoutrements were obvious, but whose infrastructure consisted of unwritten rigid social rules about who could be where with whom, when, and how. There was no clear "why" to explain all this or help me understand its impact, but I knew I felt safe being a WASP. Was that a little "racist"—just a-little I told myself.

ACT SIX. WOUNDS OF PRIVILEGE. COLLEGE AND MORE.

I went to Smith College, partly because I was NOT going to go to Vassar. My paternal grandmother who'd graduated from Vassar in the "class of aughty-aught" (1900) had lobbied for me to apply to her alma mater. I chose Smith. It was a college for women only, just as my beloved New York elementary school had been a school for girls only. I loved Smith's campus and that students lived in houses—no dorms and no sororities with all their sisterly pain. Best of all, Annie was given a scholarship and she was going there too.

SCENE FIFTEEN. WEALTH

I knew it was a privilege to go to Smith, not because I knew I was privileged, but because my father groaned out loud about the "astronomical" tuition which in 1956 was absurdly low—below $10,000 in today's dollars, plus room and board. Dad survived, and I did well and graduated in 1960.

Annie had to leave Smith after one year. Her scholarship money dwindled, and her father, PhD and the principal of a grade school, couldn't afford to pay the tuition. Our hearts were broken.

Impulsively, I told Annie that my father would pay her room and board, but she said her father would be too proud to accept. We were both right.

Annie went on to graduate from the University of Connecticut with honors. We stayed friends of course, but there was an almost indiscernible crack inside me, like a slight fracture in a bone. What was it? Guilt? No, it was the fissure of privilege. I knew how to spell that word correctly, without a *d*. Nevertheless, that extra "d" in Privi*ledge* made the word itself sound as if one could be perched on a dangerous *edge* like Humpty Dumpty.

I was learning to feel the edgy power of social privilege—the power to rent asunder, to hurt when it was supposed to help.

Despite my own father's financial worries, my family had wealth—not vast amounts of money but *wealth*, that invisible security blanket enjoyed by some and not others. It had to do with family name and security; it had to do with neighborhood, class, and family assets; it had to do with privilege and the cruel habit of ranking opportunity accordingly. It had to do with the same thing that forced southern blacks to flee their beloved homeland in order to survive.

The wealth gap had nothing to do with what I'd been brought up to value: work hard and you'll get ahead. I was learning *classism*. It even regulated neighborhoods. Annie lived literally "on the other side of the tracks." Classism, a first cousin to racism, is the fertilizer of privilege, and the pollinator of many other -isms.

Annie and I cried so hard—so very hard—when she left Smith and I stayed. My privilege bought me rank and a great education, but it did not buy me peace of mind, and it surely didn't make me feel good or superior, but rather uncomfortably exiled—whited out, in fact.

* * * *

ACT SIX. WOUNDS OF PRIVILEGE. COLLEGE AND MORE.

In college I met my first Jew. I didn't know what a Jew was. Now that is a hilarious statement. Really! It sounds absurdly anti-semitic, but I didn't know what that meant. I'd heard of THE Holocaust, but not really, if you know what I mean. As with Blacks, there were no Jews in my suburban town. I was sheltered and tragically warped.

My sheltered ignorance was appalling, not my fault, but painful anyway.

I relied on my intellectual abilities and chose academics to make my mark. I majored in Spanish, because I loved living languages and could roll my R's. It did pay off. I studied like a fiend, got good grades, was elected to Phi Beta Kappa, earned graduate degrees in time, and felt smarter than I really was. Okay, that's not fair to me, but in college I didn't yet know how to be fair to myself. I must, however, have learned about such fairness/unfairness when I'd lobbied for Carol Lee's inclusion at my party.

SCENE SIXTEEN. SOCIAL DISORGANIZATION. MY RIGHTS?

I was fascinated by the title of a college course called Social Disorganization. It promised something different. The professor, Neal DeNood, didn't stride in and slowly approach the podium with professorial dignity, but rather bounded in and hopped up on the dais. I liked him instantly. He had zip, was extraordinarily handsome, and sported a small upper-lip mustache. Almost all the other male professors were clean shaven. I'd heard someone in the religion department use the word charisma—sparkling with charm. Mr. De Nood had charisma.

"There are no rights without duties," DeNood began the first class, paused, then repeated it. I wrote that down. He elaborated on his premise until it was embarrassing—humiliating. I had never thought of this equation. I had assumed my rights were legal, externally and eternally guaranteed, personal, and secured by our constitution, or maybe Jesus, according to Sunday School. I never considered these rights to be "white."

Social DIS happened as a result of too much social unevenness. Unevenness brought revolution, sometimes war, sometimes riots and crimes, even assassinations and possibly capital punishment.

Unevenness happened when basic human rights to things like housing, education, healthcare, and economic security were *not* supported by appropriate legal, economic, medical, political, legislative, and economic structures and policies, accessible to all members of any society. Race was not even a targeted category. It was, however, a silent governor of the whole process. In a democratic society, we the people have a say in such policies, and politicians work to assure everyone these rights. *No rights without duties.*

What were *my* duties?

I had started in private school for girls only and switched to public. I was glad, thinking public would be less snobby/preppy. Students earned their place by academic merit—also money. Wealth or merit? Which? Both? For whom?

Was my privilege my right? my duty? both? neither? How much did it depend on money? For the first time it dimly occurred to me that my own skin's non-color—white—was a significant factor in social disorganization.

* * * *

During the writing of this book, I searched the Smith College archives. Neal De Nood was made a full professor in 1958. He'd started his teaching career at Smith in 1937-38, the year I was born. Safe to say he was too old for me, yet I loved his perky style. The archivist wrote that De Nood "startled his colleagues and undergraduates with his prowess as a lecturer, his unorthodox

ACT SIX. WOUNDS OF PRIVILEGE. COLLEGE AND MORE.

views, and his penchant for the sensational." He was not a professorial type.

I never forgot the no-rights-without-duties wisdom. It was inspirational—scary. He didn't mention, but implied, society's gender inequity based on not only color but race and gender.

DeNood organized a visit for our class to a women's prison in Framingham, Massachusetts. It was a shocking experience to see and hear all these furiously raging women, both black and white. I felt frightened. Helpless.

SCENE SEVENTEEN. THE CHAPLAIN

In college I gave more than one glancing thought to God, the one I'd met under a table as a young child, the God who created, tracked, and identified every sound on Earth— "to find the place that each came from." This is the image of the God who listened to my chatter about the injustice of my parent's nasty cocktail hour that excluded me. It also seemed to me that Jesus had listened to *everyone* as he traveled about, identifying rights with duties and justice with peace. But they killed him.

The next best available living resource was the college chaplain, the Rev. Mr. Richard Unsworth—another crushingly handsome object for my affection, next only to a Spanish professor, already the chosen object of my affections. Still, I thought the chaplain might have some ideas about my rights and duty questions. He agreed about Jesus. He also listened to my yearnings for religious ritual—sort of Catholic but not. Listening I already knew was God-like. Unsworth suggested that I try the Episcopal church—the very last thing I thought would help.

I'd grown up in the Presbyterian Church which in the 1940's and '50's was dry and brittle like aging parchment. I had tried those Catholics that Betty Singer sang about, and discovered at Mass, a Mystery, all in Latin. It held me in its grip. BUT, the Roman Catholic priest I talked to was a bust. He did okay about racism (not a godly thing) but he failed at sexism. Women were created to mother babies, no matter what, everlastingly! Except Mary-in-concrete statuary. I tried the Episcopal Church.

While driving my mind nuts thinking about rights, I found a rite— a ritual, a sacramental meal that required no thinking at all and engaged my whole body. In this Episcopal Church there were some requirements, but for now I brushed requirements aside, because everyone had a right to come and be fed. Intuitively, I realized that this meal could not be racist if it tried—unless of course the Church and its control issues mucked it up.

The Episcopal Church and I bonded. I met with the parish priest at St. John's in Northampton, Massachusetts. He taught me the basic creed and catechetical requirements. I knew I'd been baptized, but now it was my duty to be confirmed and join. Later I found out that my mother had grown up in the Episcopal Church, and my parents were married at St. Bartholomew's Episcopal Church in New York City. Why didn't Mom tell me? Oh yes, she was following my Presbyterian dad.

SCENE EIGHTEEN. A PSYCH. TEST

In college I'd first thought I would major in English, because I loved literature. Then I thought I'd major in Religion, because I loved God. Finally, I decided to major in Spanish, because I loved languages, could roll my R's, and had a blossoming crush on my favorite Spanish professor, a handsome poet from Spain no less. I also considered majoring in Psychology, because I needed clues about the inner workings of, well, everyone, including myself.

I took several psychology courses. One of them included some kind of a personality test, not Myers Briggs or MMPI, to identify

ACT SIX. WOUNDS OF PRIVILEGE. COLLEGE AND MORE.

personality types. I answered everything, hid nothing. The test revealed my personality type: RELIGIOUS.

A religious personality was defined as someone who tended to see things in wholes, who looked for and saw the larger picture, valuing it, in spite of, and sometimes at the expense of, contradictory details. I already knew I wasn't practical, and hated getting mired in many details. I would always be doomed to seek balance—with a larger vision always beckoning.

Spanish poetry won out.

ACT SEVEN. SPAIN.

I finished Smith in 1960. I was 21. Who decided I was an adult at 21? I certainly didn't feel of age inside. I felt unsteady, unready for the world. I should, I thought, be doing something activist about Civil Rights—march, protest, demonstrate. Maybe, but first I should go to Spain. I had a Danforth Fellowship award for graduate education. I should be with people who spoke Spanish—for real not in a classroom.

With help from my college, I located two families, one in Madrid and one in Santander, both willing to house a college graduate at reasonable rates over six weeks in the summer. I stuffed a huge suitcase with my whole wardrobe—or at least everything my mother told me would make me "presentable," her favorite word, and "sexy," my favorite word. Who knew what I'd need? Whom I'd meet? Off I went—terrified.

In one way I was escaping into the world of cultural expansion that my scholarship demanded, and in another way I was pursuing something else. What?

ACT SEVEN. SPAIN.

SCENE NINETEEN. JOB —THE GUY AND THE VISION

On the long overseas flight I read a little, stared out the tiny window, ate my snacks, and dozed. When nervous I often tried to think of a biblical character who felt as I did. I mean if stuff like this made it into ancient and holy writ, then I at least wasn't alone.

The ancient tale of Job popped in and out of my mental musings. Annoyed, I tried to push Job away. I wanted something soothing, sweet, and loaded with certainty. I didn't think I wanted to teach Spanish the way I'd seen it done.

Job was insistent, as his character already had demonstrated. He was plagued by loss, illness and trauma, ceaselessly badgered God, and all his friends and family, about his righteousness rights. He'd been good, so did he not deserve a life free of suffering, or at least less suffering, or suffering with an explanation? Didn't God, being divine and all, have a duty to explain divine policy? Job's wife suggested he curse God and die—not such a bad option, I thought. All Job's friends and experts of his day offered justifications about traditional righteousness theology: Job must have done something bad to deserve this suffering. But Job would have none of it. As I prayed and worried about my own future—all of it at once—I too badgered God. I wanted to marry and have children AND I wanted a career, a job, professional esteem.

God heard Job's nagging and at last responded with an exceptional personal tour of all Creation— with God as the tour guide no less. This impressive vision even included God's reprimand to Job's self-righteous friends. To Eliphaz of Teman, God said: "I am very angry with you and your two friends for not speaking truthfully about me as Job, my faithful one, did." (from *The Inclusive Bible*, Job 42:7-17)

Wow! Job *did* know how to pray, and he *did* trust that God listened. Once again, I remembered the God of my early childhood who had listened with steadfast care and comfort to all my complaints, and, yes, did *nothing* I wanted—at least on my timing.

Honestly, I once again felt like wanting my birthday party AND wanting Carol Lee to be there—both. I could not have both. Both, however, mattered equally to me—and also to God, I bet.

* * * *

My reverie was interrupted by the announcement that my plane was landing in Madrid.

It was early morning. I set my watch. I rehearsed in my mind how I would, in flawless Spanish, ask directions for a taxi to take me to my Madrid address.

Donde está la linea de pasajeros por . . . Right this way, Miss.

I chuckled inside: God *did* listen to Job's kvetching, did *not* solve Job's moral dilemma or grief, did *not* suggest psychotherapy, *did* show up to escort Job through *all* Creation—and airport personnel spoke English.

SCENE TWENTY. QUE HAY?

What's up? That became my favorite expression in colloquial Spanish. What's up? It covered a multitude of not-knowing-what-to-say moments, such as an invitation from a married man to join him in bed. *Qué hay*? I said, feigning ignorance and never giving thought to his potentially rising anatomy. I added in broken Spanish that in *las USA* we did not do such things—a giant falsehood, but it worked. The man withdrew.

In Spain I encountered all 'those Catholics' my mother disdained. In 1960, Spain was Roman Catholicism on steroids. Everyone was named some version of Jesus, Mary, Joseph, or all three. I spent

ACT SEVEN. SPAIN.

too much time on unpadded wooden kneelers. I made up some fable about having "bad" knees and sat to pray. I learned traditional prayers in Spanish. Sometimes they sounded as if Mary, not Jesus, was the *Messiah*. I soaked it up, fairly aching with awe. But was the Virgin the only real female presence?

Where were the men, the *señores* the fathers? Such rigid roles were, paradoxically, mimicking Roman Catholic hierarchical structures in which celibate male priests had the power to enforce a myriad of rules and roles while praying to a virginal female.

Sex had to be there, but this religion had strappingly strict rules. Emboldened and protected by such rules, I asked Paco, the younger son in my Madrid family, to take me to a bullfight. There I buried my feelings of compassion for the poor bull deep in the thrill of this national "sport." I got swept up in the roaring enthusiasm of the crowd swaying and shouting olé—over and over as the matador taunted the bull and excited the crowds, sweeping his cape back and forth. It was an orgasmic dance worthy of Ravel's "Bolero."

* * * *

Madrid, unlike New York where I'd grown up, had large plazas where people gathered for chats and drinks. In *las USA* we squished every ounce of concrete sidewalk together, leaving minimal public space for social time. Post-siesta and pre-dinner in Spain there was something akin to a "cocktail hour." I waved my hand to call for *cerveza* (beer) or *Cuba libre* (rum and coke) and a *merienda* (snack). Exhausted and liberated, I found my way home by 10 p.m. for the main meal, served by *chicas* or *chachas* (young girl maid-live-in servants) who kept removing plates out and other plates in. I felt I must be almost the size of my bloated suitcase by now. So what!

Following my mother's instructions, I bought a mantilla for my wedding, just in case I got married to Bill. For now I just needed to feel loved by a flesh and blood man. I prayed that virgin prayer daily, and let myself fall in love with Pepé who carried both his father's and his mother's last names. He kissed me and proposed lifelong commitment. I kissed him back, refused his proposal, and cried all the way home on the plane. Mine were the tears of unknowing. Where did I belong—wrong sex, wrong color, wrong religion, wrong race?

ACT EIGHT. INDEPENDENCE? RACISM-S.

Independence is a very important value, right? We are the "United" States, right? A goal of life itself was independence, right? For everyone, right? Still, to be independent you had to be healthfully dependent first, right? Then you had to make sure everyone had the same independence, didn't you?

I was now ready to attach an S to my racism—racismS. I had experienced sexISM, alongside genderISM, alongside ethnocentrISM (ethnocentricity). It was the 1960s and everyone, regardless of their skin color or country of origin, *should* be INdependent, right? What again was inalienable?

SCENE TWENTY-ONE. LOVE AND MARRIAGE?

Bill Brakeman and I became engaged. Engaged? I'd heard friends talk about being "hooked" on a food or on booze. Was marriage a trap, or was it a sacrament called Holy Matrimony? I wanted both.

Bill was not yet graduated from college so we waited, and while we did I romanticized. Shared love was like a beautiful seasonal painting ablaze with leaves of many colors, just as love has many moods and takes many shapes. Marriage vows preserved that love in the same way that a frame preserves a beautiful painting. Bill gave me a beautiful engagement ring with a tiny sparkling diamond in it.

* * * *

I used the Danforth grant I'd received to further my education as a teacher to rent a small apartment in Northampton while I taught freshman Spanish at Smith College. Honestly, I hated the traditional way languages were taught. Grammar ruled with memorizing as its methodology.

I audited a French class in which the professor spoke nothing but French. I loved it. Of course! It was taught exactly as children learn by absorption and immersion. I also took Russian, a more difficult undertaking because the alphabet was, well, foreign-er than Greek. The professor spoke Russian to us, but we also had to memorize an alphabet and repeat lots of words and phrases. He was a humorous man who wore a boot-shoe to support his club foot. We could hear him coming a mile away. I loved these immersive experiences.

I met regularly with a Spanish professor. Under her guidance I wrote a thesis entitled: "The Role of the Priest in the Spanish Novel." It was amazing how intrusive clergy could be—also quite amusing that I chose this topic.

All these positive experiences strung together like rosary beads. I longed for more learning, so I used the rest of my Danforth towards a Master of Arts in Spanish language and literature at Columbia University.

I could say "I do" in love *and* in marriage. Could I also be a good wife *and* a good mother of children *and* follow my own professional ambitions?

ACT EIGHT. INDEPENDENCE? RACISM-S.

I should never have read Betty Friedan's *The Feminine Mystique*, (1963). Therein was one more ISM to threaten my already overloaded pyramid of -isms now including feminISM?

I wept—not from feeling like a failure, but from the sorrow that accompanies deep foreboding.

SCENE TWENTY-TWO. LOVE *AND* AWAKENING *AND* THE SIXTIES

Bill and I rented our tiny first apartment, in uptown Manhattan. I went to Columbia to get my M.A. in Spanish language and literature while Bill commuted to his job in Connecticut. Thanks to my fearless nagging, Bill's natural good nature, my tiny homemaking efforts, like meatloaf or macaroni, and failed coitus interruptus, we'd conceived our first child, Beverley Ann Brakeman, born in 1963, followed in 1964 by a second daughter, Jill Barlow Brakeman. We loved those names, and each other, as we pored over naming books, laughing at some of the many choices, we vetoed, especially my attraction to Amalie from a book I'd read. Bill vetoed that, and we settled on Jill who later expressed gratitude to her dad for his veto.

With pride and joy I watched my belly swell, my graduate work pay off, and my worries grow.

I knew I wasn't racist, because I had felt no fear at all when I'd walked back and forth to classes at Columbia—way up-town—and later, fearlessly, took the train back to Connecticut from 125th Street in Harlem, a district where black people lived. Either I was naively white, or I just wasn't afraid of black people.

My first jolting awareness of our racist/whiteist suburban culture came, ironically after we purchased a house of our own in Darien, Connecticut, the town where we'd met and where grandparents lived. According to Rosalind Russell's rendering of the line "the

Arian from Darien" in the 1958 Broadway show, *Auntie Mame*, I could be Aryan. I had no clear idea what that meant, except that it had something to do with Hitlerian policies, and referred to anyone from *Darien* as an uptight purist prude. I was definitely NOT that uptight. Besides, I didn't know any Jews, and I wasn't racist enough, I hoped.

* * * *

Bill and I knew something about how to get education, jobs, income, and babies, but practically nothing about how to nurture each other *and* our marriage.

* * * *

By 1967, our third child, Robert William, III, the requisite male heir with "the third" after his name, was born. Two happenings jolted me awake.

1. I went to the pharmacy and whispered to the pharmacist that I wanted to buy some "Spartans" to which he replied: "Miss, I think you mean Trojans" Miss?
2. I pulled up to a Darien neighbor's house to pick something up. The door was opened by a black woman, probably their maid, and our four-year-old daughter who was with me asked *"What was that?"*

This four-year-old child wasn't racist, just innocent. We were safely ensconced in a *white-ist* culture, the pain of which had been laid bare by a small child.

SCENE TWENTY-THREE. SALVATION?

Trying to save a marriage is not the same thing as saving love itself. I loved our children without condition, yet had no idea how also to love myself without losing myself. I wondered if religions

ACT EIGHT. INDEPENDENCE? RACISM-S.

felt the same way, because they seemed to be blinded by rules that bound Love into a strait jacket. Wasn't I supposed to have some kind of guardian angel?

Bill, beset with breadwinner—*itis*, took a job down south in Anniston, Alabama. THE SOUTH! At least it was in the NORTHERN south. AND there were *two* Episcopal churches in town.

I tried the uptown church nearest to us. I was repelled by a big bold sign out front: WHITES ONLY. The downtown parish was, yes, ALL BLACK. I went downtown where the worship style was Baptist. They danced and called out many Hallelujahs. I felt like an outlaw.

So I stayed home, cleaned my house ruthlessly and met a friend—the next-door maid. She was black, called me *Honey*, and became my best friend. She was tall and majestic and her name was LOveenia—yes, not LAvinia. She crossed over from next door to visit, and gave me cleaning lessons: "Honey, y'all cleaning that floor too much. Ease up, girl." I felt beloved.

Perhaps I was just as racist as any faithful southerner? Or possibly, there was no such thing as THE south. Racists lived everywhere—even in medicine! The gynecologist shrugged when I asked him for help. I knew the sprongy thing I used did not work. Bill's new job was beyond disappointing to him. We nursed our sorrows with Scotch.

- Our kids developed southern accents
- The nursery school had a graduation at which was played, yes, Elgar's *Pomp and Circumstance*
- Neighborhood amusements included local boys bribing our daughters to show their underpants. I didn't ask for details, but they both came home with nickels.
- Daughter #2 taught herself to read *before* her older sister.

- Bill discovered a new engineering phenomenon called cable television.
- I got pregnant AGAIN with our fourth.
- We moved AGAIN—at first back to Connecticut, "homeland." Safe, yet . . . I could only bake so many chocolate chip cookies, get so many degrees, worry so much, before another century rolled over into THE seventies.

Bill had engineering skills. My now retired dad had money. My mother had the passion to start a family commune. I had the womb great with child. Bill and Dad schemed a new business venture in the field of cable television! All together we moved north from Darien to settle in another "foreign" country called Collinsville in northwest Connecticut, specifically North Canton where, according to Dad's lawyer, the labor would be cheaper for their new business venture called Cable Ten, which sadly failed, in part because the business partners had radically differing business management styles.

My younger sister and her husband joined the family migration. I never loved her more than for following along, bringing cousins/playmates. At the same time I cringed at all this family togetherness and the amount of survival drinking Bill and I were doing together.

ACT NINE. THE SEVENTIES

How much change was too much change all at once? At such times the highest spiritual gift is HOPE.

SCENE TWENTY-FOUR. NEW BABY. NEW RECTOR. NEW SORROW.

John Thomas Brakeman, was born in November, 1970, at Hartford Hospital where a sadistic OB/GYN doctor told me: "You have an old and tired uterus." That was just after he administered Scopolamine, a hallucinogenic drug also known as Devil's Breath. It caused me to see fierce wild animals and other nightmarish images all over the walls and ceiling. Would God save ME now?

Bill had invested his time and talent in a new business in Stratford, Connecticut. This was his dream. By the time John was six, I pursued my own dream and went to Yale Divinity School (YDS). I aspired to be a priest, despite having been turned down by the diocesan screening committee who said God had already "ordained" me a mother, forever at home baking chocolate chip cookies. They called it a "dual vocation."

By 1978, Dick Simeone was the new rector of Trinity parish in Collinsville. An odd energy vibrated between us. I ignored it.

Unexpectedly and tragically in 1979, my youngest sister Jeanie died after brain aneurysm surgery. Suddenly, I could hardly breathe. It took a while before I got the right diagnosis and medication for asthma.

Once again, I turned to prayer and the Bible. Where *was* God? How *did* biblical people keep trying and crying as they moved about seeking a homeland? No one in the Bible ever gave up, they just got pregnant, trusted God, and multiplied—just as we had.

SCENE TWENTY-FIVE. *DOMINUS FLEVIT*

All I did was cry. Why *was* I doing this?

At this time of sorrow and impending life changes, I wondered a lot about Jesus. He was supposed to be THE Savior of everyone, right? Now I needed lessons on how to have wild feelings, not get pregnant, be a mother, initiate divorce, and follow Jesus, in case he had salvation wrapped. I remembered that once, only once on record, Jesus wept. It showed me he was human— compassionate, and definitely not racist because he'd converted to Christianity and favored loving the worst of neighbors.

Sorrowing matters. When Jesus heard that his dear friend Lazarus had died, he wept. His grief and love showed up all at once—hopelessly and helplessly. Whether a miracle happened to restore Lazarus or not, Jesus's powerfully human tears stood out. He also wept about the impending destruction of Jerusalem. (Luke 19:41-44) .The church in Israel that now memorializes such grief is shaped like a teardrop and called *Dominus Flevit* (The Lord Wept).

ACT NINE. THE SEVENTIES

SCENE TWENTY-SIX. SPACIOUS HEARTS.
LOVE *AND* DIVORCE.

Good humor, deep caring, an attraction I would never discount, and the blessing of our four remarkable children had sustained me and Bill over twenty years of marriage. We both fell in love with drinking. He fell in love with his business success. I fell in love with myself as a woman, took my first tiny job as a reporter of local news, discovered lesbian sex, and my attraction to the secrets of the altar. In time we both fell in love with other people.

We divorced in 1982. When we came out of the courthouse we hugged. I chose to receive alimony instead of child support, a decision my attorney disliked, because it meant that I would pay taxes on alimony while Bill got a tax break. I saw this as my tiny way of contributing to the children's higher education. Bill never missed an alimony payment and paid for all their college educations. We both would soon remarry, yet I suspect that neither of us deeply understood what exactly made our marriage fail, even though both of us knew that it had to end.

Many years later in 2007 at the Baptism of a grandchild, Bill and I met for a coffee date —in the same diner named Driftwood where we'd had our very first date in 1955. We could blame certain things but would never fully understand the whole. Nevertheless, for all of it, our children, and all our shared memories and humor, I remain grateful.

The human heart, I was learning, is a spacious vessel, capable of holding many loves and many pains, an infinity of feelings, and plenty of Soul freedom, the gift of Divinity to us all.

ACT TEN. IN THE DARK WITH GLIMMERS IN GRIEF

I was learning that the kind of deep personal and emotional engagement required for marriage, or fluency in a foreign language, or authentic grieving *might* be THE way to address *all* "racismS." It *might* be the way to love someone else and not lose myself, *might* be a healer of both whiteouts *and* blackouts?

SCENE TWENTY-SEVEN. ETHER

When we all moved to North Canton, my parents invited Ethel, a black woman who had cleaned for them to come live with them in their North Canton house. The way she said her name made it sound like "Etha." She came to be called Ether. She ironed every thing in sight and cleaned, and had her own room. But Ether *never* dined with the family. Why? It might have been her choice, or a silent race rule. I wondered.

I could explain who this was to my children, but I wondered whether the role of "maid" had a racist tinge. Was it like being Fred who served "more potatoes" but never sat with us at my grandparents' dining table?

I knew that if I ever saw Carol Lee again I'd invite her to eat with us.

SCENE TWENTY-EIGHT. THE RELATIONAL WAY, A NEW PSYCHOLOGY

I read the ground-breaking work *Toward a New Psychology of Women* (1976) by social activist psychologist, Dr. Jean Baker Miller. I understood that the psychological wellbeing of a woman was derived from mutually growth-fostering relationships.

Miller lists five good things that happen when you create, or are fortunate enough to find yourself in, a mutually respectful relationship: 1) *zest* for life and energy that comes from being fully seen and loved, both; 2) greater *creativity/productivity*; 3) increased *self esteem*; 4) *clarity* in thought, word and deed; 5) *desire for more* such relationships.

"Mutually," to me, meant that my needs were as important as others'. I could even be mutual with a child. For example, a certain five year old wanted to linger in the toy section of the supermarket, but it was also time to go home for supper. I saw a temper tantrum brewing, so I took a breath, squatted to his level, and asked him what he wanted. This made him stop to think, and breathe: "I just like seeing all the toys and maybe play with some. They let you, you know." I nodded and told him my need: "Great idea. Can we plan it for tomorrow, because right now I have to go home to start making our supper? Okay, bud?" I stayed near him as he considered, then agreed.

This relational way of life requires spacious hearts. If you lived this way, you couldn't be racist or sexist or classist. But I could be *mutual* with men or blacks or poor people in slums, begging on the streets? I didn't know their needs. I knew they were there for some reason. I could be generous, let go of my assumptions, and, sometimes have a conversation. There is always a story about such coming-aliveness.

ACT TEN. IN THE DARK WITH GLIMMERS IN GRIEF

SCENE TWENTY-NINE. THE REV. RICHARD (DICK) JOHN SIMEONE

The first time I met Dick Simeone was on the phone. It was 1977. I was on the parish search committee at Trinity Episcopal Church in Collinsville, CT. I was calling him to ask if some of us on the search committee could pay a visit that next Sunday to the parish in Palmyra, Maine where he was a Rector and priest. It was Labor Day weekend. As I told him the reason for my call, I inwardly grinned. What a colossally dumb thing to do on a holiday. But this priest was cheery and charming, totally confident. Our visit went well, and by l978, Dick Simeone accepted our parish's call to serve as our clergy. I didn't know it back then, but I was falling in love.

Much later Dick would tell me that he had fallen in love with my voice on the phone. I thought it should have been the first time he *saw* me in my dusty pink top. Whatever evolved between us wasn't immediately romantic or sexual. It was a depth of knowing that never stopped.

Much later as well, I would tell him that I fell in love with him for the first time when I saw him functioning as a priest at the altar in this small parish in Maine with very few worshipers in the congregation that day. Neither the reduced size of the congregation nor the fact that there were visitors from afar fazed "Father" Simeone who reassured and instructed a small boy acolyte about lighting the altar candles before he followed the boy who, with unstable yet undisguised pride, carried a cross three times his size into the sanctuary.

Father Simeone stood behind the altar and celebrated the Holy Eucharist in grand style, as if it were Easter or some high holy day in a cathedral. To this priest, every Sunday was Easter. If I were the swooning type I would have swooned. This was the kind of priest I wanted to be. This was how to praise, yes, Divinity itself in all its many shapes and images. This must be "high church." I loved it—fell right into love.

I believe my dad was quite sold as well, because he called Simeone "our boy" and would soon himself be received into the Episcopal Church. I wept when I saw him kneel before the bishop for his blessing.

* * * *

I later discovered that the Bishop of Connecticut had voted *against* the 1976 Episcopal General Convention's vote to open priestly ordination to women. At our interview with Simeone after the church service, the first question I asked was: "What do you think about the ordination of women to the priesthood?"

He delivered an enthusiastic little sermonette by which I understood he was for it. Only later did he tell me that originally he had been against it—territorial rights and rites of the long-reigning sexist exclusivity of the male priesthood, I suppose. At least I knew he knew about being in the dark and he wasn't sexist.

School has always been salvific for me. In the divinity school I grew closer to myself and to the God I'd met as a child. Studying theology was electrifying.

I was graduated from YDS in 1982 with no job, no promise, no ordination, little self-pride, divorced from Bill, and filled with a burning desire to be free and to go wild, which I did. I was turned away again for ordination by the Church, and thrown back into the outer darkness.

Dick Simeone believed in me and believed that I would be ordained. He encouraged me not to quit. I thought he must be nuts.

* * * *

ACT TEN. IN THE DARK WITH GLIMMERS IN GRIEF

As I grieved, I hung onto the ideas of two theologians I'd studied in seminary. These old boys saved my spiritual life. One was Danish theologian/philosopher/poet, Soren Kierkegaard (1813-1855) who believed in free will and wrote about the spiritual struggle he called "the leap of faith" by which one stayed in touch with God's supremacy *and* one's own will and freedom at the same time.

The other theologian whose work I'd read for the required course called Systematic Theology was Professor John Macquarrie (1919-2007), a Scottish-born Anglican theologian and priest who summarized the image of God as *letting be and drawing near* —both at once.

Years later I met John Macquarrie in person at Holy Cross Monastery. After taking a deep breath, I signed up for an individual session. When I entered the meeting room I sat down across from him and burst into tears. He waited in silence. Then he listened to my blubbering story of grief and rejection and my sins. He made no judgment; nor did he give me advice. He just listened with care.

* * * *

Throughout this entire time of my searching for God, myself, love, truth, and vocation, my four growing children carried on with their own precious lives in the midst of my mid-life insanity.

SCENE THIRTY. WHAT ABOUT SEX-ISM?

Sexism became one of my "racismS" while I struggled through the elaborate ordination processes in the patriarchal Episcopal Church—committee after committee, rejection after rejection—all because I could not, in their judgment, be a mother *and* a priest.

After fierce lamenting, I purchased a Crockpot whose sweating and simmering accompanied me as I plunged into Bioenergetic therapy where I awakened my fascinatingly embodied self, anatomy and all. Imagine praying naked!

All my rage at the Church of Men Only, and my own mother's teachings about motherhood being the *only* worthwhile vocation, were stored in my carnality, which exploded. There really is life below the belt.

Dick Simeone never put me down. He listened. Soon we broke one of the Big Ten "thou shalt nots." A well-meaning church lady ratted us out, and the newly elected Connecticut bishop sent us putative "church criminals" to see another bishop for his opinion. He was eloquently forgiving and offered us this odd old wisdom: "If Christ is in your relationship it will prevail." I laughed at first. Then I panicked. Was Christ a peeping tom?

ACT ELEVEN. EMERGENCE INTO THE LIGHT. COMING ALIVE.

How ironic it is that sin is often *both* the way to fall in love with the self, *and* the way to stay in love with Divinity. Sin is whatever separates anyone from the goodness in God, self, and neighbors. Life in a Whiteout is fertile ground for sin-filled "racism." So is life in a Blackout.

Prayer keeps this grand vision of divine goodness alive and intact on the ground. Prayer can be formal and informal, communal and alone—all my longings, confusions, desires, and needs, counted, whether I got the prayed-for results or not. There is no such thing as prayer-ism.

SCENE THIRTY-ONE. WORD AND SACRAMENT

There must also be a rule book for guidance—a darn good and holy one. There is: *The Book of Common Prayer. According to the use of The Episcopal Church.(BCP)*

"Just read it," Dick said.

The BCP *Preface*, written way back in 1789 by an old white man named Cranmer, defines *all* "rules" as flexible and subject to ratification as deemed appropriate. I'd skipped over it.

Dick said, just read it! So I did.

It is a most valuable part of that blessed "liberty wherewith Christ hath made us free," that in his worship different forms and usages may without offence be allowed, provided the substance of the Faith be kept entire: and that, in every Church, what cannot be clearly determined belong to Doctrine must be referred to Discipline; and therefore, may be altered, abridged, enlarged, amended, or otherwise, or otherwise disposed of, as may seem most convenient for the edification of the people" according to the various exigencies of times and occasions."

Well, I'll be damned. I could be an exigency! Once again, there was a book when I needed it.

* * *

How about sacraments—ritual acts and words that make things holy—like bread and wine and water, also races, genders and sins—even needy sinners like me? I know it doesn't make sense, but what does—really?

The Sacrament of Reconciliation of a Penitent is when a priest places hands on your one small bowed head and pronounces forgiveness for, and absolution of, personal sins. Tell it out loud? Well, yes, but not to the rooftops, or the whole House of Bishops.

It was my time to receive this sacrament. I chose as my confessor a priest I'd known in the chaplaincy training program. I knew he could be dignified and detached enough to exercise this rite as if he had never known me and had not already heard all my confessional tears and woes in our chaplaincy supervision group.

ACT ELEVEN. EMERGENCE INTO THE LIGHT. COMING ALIVE.

I trusted him. Good thing because I was about to spill my guts all over him.

I knelt and bowed my head—the same body language of the ordination rite when *many* hands are laid on an ordinand's head as *she* kneels before a bishop who prays and asks God, through Christ and the Holy Spirit, to make *her* a priest in the Church. Could God see who was under those hands? Ordination is a solemn, heavy-handed and terrifying sacrament of ministry, open to those who, frankly, dare to pursue it. WARNING: if you do it too often it becomes narcissistic— poor me-itis.

Such a mighty moment was facilitated without rewriting the whole rule book but by the simple italicization of the gender pronouns after the rules changed. Hilarious!

The Reconciliation of a Penitent is one of the most intimate sacramental acts imaginable, precisely because it is *not* overused. I have only received it once at my request and according to my own readiness. Afterwards, I felt lighter in body and soul. I'd experienced soul nudity.

When the sacramental process was completed, my confessor rose and removed his official priestly stole. I stood up. We hugged.

SCENE THIRTY-TWO. WHAT ABOUT BIBLICAL CHARACTERS?

I recalled a writing workshop at Holy Cross Monastery led by writer and spiritual director Madeleine L'Engle. She said: "Pick someone in Holy Scripture you think might have felt angry and then write about it." Then she left the meeting room. I felt angry, abandoned, ashamed. I just wanted answers! The snake in Genesis popped into my mind. This poor old snake had been blamed for the whole messy process of sin in the world—a cosmic scapegoat.

All the snake did was tell the truth: you won't die if you eat that fruit, not an apple by the way.

I gave voice to the snake in a story called "The Asp's Lament" which ended up years later in my first published book. Thanks to Madeleine's jumpstart, I wrote more about biblical characters trapped in the darkness of injustices imposed from without, like racismS. No one is born racist.

ACT TWELVE. RIGHTS AND DUTIES REVISITED

It wasn't my "right" to have divinity within me either. Fine, BUT I still could not fit myself and my femaleness into the traditional, tightly woven Christian theological scheme in which God was *He, Him, His;* Jesus the Christ was also *He, Him, His,* and likewise the Holy Spirit! Jesus was also Jewish! Some people even thought he was Roman Catholic!

"Oh, you have to find a Jesuit if you really want to know Jesus well," said a woman who was in my chaplaincy training program.

SCENE THIRTY-THREE. MY JESUIT

I found a Jesuit spiritual director by the name of Pierre Wolff. He was from France with the accent to prove it. This part would have pleased my mother, a certified francophile. Pierre practiced his ministry at Mercy Center in Madison, Connecticut, a place I grew to love. Whenever there were introductions Pierre always introduced himself as "Pierre Wolff, France."

Pierre guided me through the Spiritual Exercises of St Ignatius of Loyola, an intensive process through which I was open and opened to Jesus, the "guy" of Nazareth whose life, words, and actions led me deeply into Divinity Incarnate—in Jesus's flesh and mine.

Pierre's coaching, his own irritation with Rome's negative attitude about women priests, alongside the insouciance of my simmering Crockpot, helped me wait, albeit impatiently—for the Episcopal Church to catch up. It was the 1980s now, and women, since 1976, could be ordained to the Episcopal priesthood. I waited.

Institutions can be bullish—stubbornly thick-skinned while blindly certain of their righteousness and power. Rules, no matter how sound structurally, function like straight jackets when they generate fear that drowns creativity and paralyzes soul-muscle.

* * * *

On September 10, 1988, I officiated at the marriage of Pierre and the lovely Mary Morgan, a sister of Mercy. It was the first marriage rite at which I officiated after I was—finally—ordained priest in March, 1988. I still do not know how I managed this marriage as such a brand new priest. I did it for Pierre who gave me Jesus for real. The required pre-marital counseling was a role switch of vast proportions.

To prevent error or passing out, I received close, word-by-word counseling from Dick. What page was Holy Matrimony on again? We rehearsed. Dick called out the moves: "Now, say these words carefully, slowly, correctly. It's the moment Jesus jumps into the bread!" "You mean the Christ, don't you?"

A female Roman Catholic, a guest at the wedding, expressed awe that "the priest had dangling earrings." In time, Pierre, under the tutelage of The Rt. Rev. Arthur E. Walmsley, the same bishop who had ordained me, left his Roman Catholic church and become an Episcopal priest himself. I was honored to preach at Pierre's burial service.

ACT TWELVE. RIGHTS AND DUTIES REVISITED

* * * *

Who knows exactly what grounds us, individually and collectively, while simultaneously transporting us into wonderment at the countless ways the divine Spirit reveals things brand-new and same-old at once? God has a right to reveal the new, and we have a duty to contemplate *all* things anew, occasion by occasion. We Americans should also stop using racist labels like "Asian" and "Black" yet never "white"!

My Jesuit taught me that only *one* name—LOVE—should be used for Divinity. *We come from Love, We go to Love. Every day we walk in Love.* To follow Love for me meant to let go of myself too.

SCENE THIRTY-FOUR. MY RIGHTS?

I was thrilled with my very first paycheck from the weekly paper The Farmington Valley Herald where I was a stringer, that is, paid by the column inch. Only once did I slip into editorializing with an opinion of my own. That opinion evoked a raging letter to the editor about me and my opinion. I did not get fired but was soon promoted to Assistant Managing Editor. This meant I could occasionally write features, articles about fascinating special events or people. It also meant that I would write headlines—the most fun because they were constricted by space and each one absolutely had to catch hold of the soul of the article.

By now I was married and divorced, remarried and ordained, and supposedly mature. It was a time when I was privileged simply to BE white AND in the UPPER middle class, through no fault of my own. Black women *had* to work at a job for money, simply to make sure their children didn't die of starvation.

Did I have a right to want something more or different? I had already failed at parish ministry. Yes, but rarely without guilt, and it wasn't Betty Friedan's fault. Did I have a duty to advocate for myself? That too, but not without guilt, and it wasn't Gloria Steinem's fault. Did I pray ceaselessly? Yes, I learned that God was not going to accomplish this for me, *also* that God never abandoned me even when the Church did. Jesus the Christ did not die exclusively to free straight white men!

I had been wanton and wild and, laughingly, both at once. Jesus healed whomever came in sight, even on occasion stopping to get proper consent forms, HIPAA or not. He often asked people what they wanted even if it looked obvious. Nor did he waste time obsessing about divinity or humanity. He had the right to be both at once. Did I?

SCENE THIRTY-FIVE. WHAT ABOUT CHURCH RIGHTS?

All this religion. All this prayer. All this church. All these beautiful rites and rituals and songs held me in their grip. Ritual beauty transcends intellectual comprehension. I'd wanted to be closer to this sacramental mystery Holy Communion or Eucharist regularly—BUT, following the required traditional route toward ordination, followed by the traditional route of the parish priest proved complicated.

There was, I soon discovered, much more to being a parish priest than presiding at the altar. Parish ministry in practice felt more like being a CEO and a CFO in charge of a small business mostly dependent on volunteerISM, subject to the whims and ways and finances of its members, who pledged whatever they chose to afford and opened a daycare center for tots who paid! This meant training lay leaders to understand themselves as ministers, making sure there was enough money to afford an excellent music director who mastered the organ, a job tantamount to managing divinity-in-orgasm, and supervising it all.

ACT TWELVE. RIGHTS AND DUTIES REVISITED

Parish priesting was a helluva job, also riddled with *sexism*—better suited to straight white men with no hormones! To supplement my miniature paycheck, I followed my training in pastoral counseling and chaplaincy, and became a female "Willie Loman" permanently on the road in a blizzard.

Dick explained to me that there was a difference between being a rector (administrator) and being a priest (sacramental). I didn't see much difference.

* * * *

God, aka Holy Spirit, shot me a memory from a college course, called *Ethics*. A really ancient female Ethics professor, Miss Smith no less, mounted the podium with effort. She hung onto the lectern and posed this question: *Which is more important in making decisions, motives or consequences?* Write an essay with your answers for the next class." The next class was two days away. Was there a "right" answer? I sided quickly with *consequences*, thinking I could flunk out if I didn't comply—within two days.

Nevertheless, I remember the brainstorm this question set off inside me, and still does.

Motives and consequences could overlap, especially in acts of simple creative gratitude, like worship—art to enliven spiritual delight all round.

But was worship racist? Or was it simply a matter of style and culture and habit? Blacks worshipped with loud vivacity, and Whites preferred stiff quietude. Birdsong can be worship as grand as the huge Mormon Tabernacle choir, a single owl, a Gospel Choir, a little girl marching about crooning Handel's Hallelujah chorus, or the murmuring hum of prayers everywhere. Surround-sound!

I was motivated to create lively worship—*and* receive a pay check. Silently, I considered that the Holy Spirit Herself with all her mobility, depth, and breadth just might have a gender the same as mine.

SCENE THIRTY-SIX. THE PERFECT PAYING JOB?

I turned to the want ads and looked under the C's How often does a church advertise in the want ads? There was an ad for a Chaplain at a newly established treatment center in Bloomfield, Connecticut. I was given an interview with the Clinical Director at BlueRidge Alcohol and Drug Treatment Center, was hired as a part-time Chaplain—humorously, because, when asked, I told the clinical director that my Jesus had dirt under his fingernails.

At BlueRidge I thrived. I learned that addiction was a disease to be treated, not a moral failure to be corrected, nor a sin to be punished. I learned that Whites and Blacks suffer the same! The patients and their stories taught me the rest. I worked there from 1984 to1990 when BlueRidge folded, mostly because of lack of funding, assisted I bet by racist AND sexist assumptions about substance abusers.

I knew alcoholics could be female or black, yet I'd observed that women and blacks suffered the most condemnation. White middle class affluence reigned over medical intelligence. ClassISM + racISM + sexISM—lethal bundle of judgmentalISM. Recovery programs help, not just because of anonymity, but because they advocate telling your story.

I risked telling the patients that one of my uncles, a wealthy white business executive became so annoyingly preachy about Alcoholics Anonymous that I wished he'd get a drink and shut up! The patients laughed uproariously. I did not tell them I too drank too much, partly because I thought it might save my shaky marriage.

ACT TWELVE. RIGHTS AND DUTIES REVISITED

Alcoholics told me they resented the domineering whiteist patriarchal culture that silently guaranteed unjust racist judgments. Women were judged more harshly, and mothers the worst.

When in 1988 I was ordained priest, my BlueRidge "congregation" cheered. I was so darn proud of my stiff white uncomfortable clerical collar, that I flicked my forefinger on its stiffness while saying a quick prayer that I would not get stiffly white too.

ACT THIRTEEN. ONGOING FORMATION.

I'd fallen in love with Jesus the man called Christ. Christ, *Kyrios* in Greek, meant The Anointed One. But were we not ALL potential "christs" with a small *c*? Did one have to be a male Christian to be a christ? And why was this ONE Almighty God *always* called Father? AND *always* assumed to be white and exclusively TRANSCENDENT?

Many BlueRidge patients applauded when I reminded them that black people invented Jazz and Gospel choirs, and women invented nursing—all to praise the *same* Creator of all.

The divinity school campus was high on a hill overlooking the rest of Yale campus, as if Divinity were always looking and speaking down from above—not to mention all those piercing phallic steeples. It was so racist/sexist/patriarchal that I laughed.

How exactly did God get down and in?

SCENE THIRTY-SEVEN. ALL-FROM-ABOVE EXCLUSIVELY?

I grew into my vocation by remembering.

ACT THIRTEEN. ONGOING FORMATION.

Once in junior high school a teacher posed the following question to a bunch of upturned but blank-faced seventh graders: Who was the greatest man in the world and why? I knew enough not to put down my father, which wouldn't have been quite true anyway, as much as I adored him. I wrote down Abraham Lincoln. Why? He freed the slaves of course. My answer was void of historical complexities, but the teacher accepted it anyway. Why? Well, there was no freakin' *right* answer!

I became a student of small details, such as the act of mercy one of the Roman guards at Jesus's execution by piercing Jesus's side as he hung there. Why? So Jesus would not have to suffer the *slow* agony of death by suffocation.

Lincoln hoped to seed a country, Jesus a new way of being. Both were killed for telling the truth, and neither one had slipped into racism or exclusionary rhetoric along the torturous way of promoting a unitive vision. Both men posed a challenge to injustices, and neither got blinded by a blizzard or a blackout. Both were scapegoats! Both were assassinated.

By 2020, I would read: "Lincoln will not return from the dead, even as a ghost, but his broadly balanced democratic pluralism may be all there is to rescue us yet again." (*New Yorker,* 9/28/20, Adam Gopnik "Better Angel. An Abraham Lincoln of His Time, and Ours.")

Such a vision of egalitarian politics felt futile, and yet I needed a Christ who never gave up—Hope no matter what, a Divinity whose immanent breath became my own.

SCENE THIRTY-EIGHT. SOWER PARABLE REVISITED. READY, SET, GO?

This sower went into a field to sow seeds. Of course he did. It was his daily job in the agricultural culture of ancient times. And of course some soil was fertile and some not.

What each of us *really* wants to know is: what about my own soil? Is *my* soil, *my* soul, *my* parish, *my* country the best? We could compete ourselves to death. The Sower? Sows.

> *Sow me, Sower*
> *Sow your seeds.*
>
> *In the beginning, I am fertile—flirty, fruitful, foxy*
> *Any seed is mine. Every seed bears fruit.*
>
> *In the middle, I try out soil-types—obsess about my own—until*
> *I harden against any seed,*
>   *waste seeds, ignore others,*
> *arid with indifference,*
>   *thinned by busyness and grief,*
>   *bloated with pride or affluence*
> *The Sower deftly sows—all seeds mine, all soils me.*
>
> *At the ending time*
> *I don't care—nor lie nor fake nor die*
>   *—nor try to be sower seed or soil alone*
>
> *Sower, seed, and soil—just so.*
>
> *Sower, sower, double my order. Thank you.*

ACT FOURTEEN. LEAPINGS

It took me a while to dare to know what I really wanted. The thought of quiet insanity, something like "the death of a housewife" jolted me. The shock awakened me, accompanied by the slam of school books on the kitchen table and a young voice: "Hey Mom, I'm going over to So-and So's house, ok? She didn't wait for my answer. I was not indispensable.

SCENE THIRTY-NINE. POWERING UP

Yes! I went up to the tippy-top of a very high peak called Talcott mountain overlooking the Farmington Valley in Connecticut. There I got strapped into a harness—and, with minimal instruction, leaped. Suicidal? I remembered the landing instructions and where I would set down. I did not remember or care how old I was, nor that I might die. Had I told anyone where I would be?

Yes! I took a pinch-hitter course in flying a small plane myself, because Bill flew a small plane. My instructor was a judge somewhere in the Farmington Valley. He was the calmest most collected person I had ever met. I loved the power surge of a take-off. The most terrifying part was landing. It looked as if the ground were much closer that it actually was, as if it came up to meet me—or grab me to its bosom in a crash! I got the knack of it, but had no urge to become a pilot!

Yes! I became more involved in local Episcopal church politics. With all the chutzpah of a newly charged and angry aspirant for ordination in a Church whose Canon Laws prohibited the likes of me, I leaped into church politics and was elected the Dean of our North Central deanery. Then I leaped into seminary at Yale Divinity School and commuted from North Canton to New Haven. I made sure to pick courses that met at times when my children would be in school.

Yes! Such decisive moments helped me to retrieve my own energy from deep inside and to overcome the blindness of whitism. Carol Lee and other black people had doors slammed against them all the time and they soldiered on anyway. I had done the same! I mean, after all, I wasn't Burt Lancaster waiting for his own wings to fly him out of Alcatraz, for chrissake? This, my dad's favorite oath, reminded me that I should know more about this Christ—more than all the syrupy Sunday School stories about a stuck-in-the-manger savior baby. Jesus grew up, didn't he?

Many of my *seeds* and *wings* came from stories of courage in the Bible.

SCENE FORTY. CHOICES OF PAIN AND GAIN

Choice by choice, I devoured my freedom—moving, leap by leap, away from traditional and expected roles. I could have blamed the 70s or Betty Friedan and Gloria Steinem, but that would be cheap grace. I took it anyway. Slowly feminism took shape and was established as one of my "-ismS."

My four children were exhilarated by the lack of excessive parental supervision *and* scared by too much maternal abandonment—paternal as well.

ACT FOURTEEN. LEAPINGS

My desire to stand up behind the altar table not crouch beneath it drove me on. I wanted to be a woman-in-the-flesh up front, not a stone female statue draped with sorrowful looks and roses. I decided as well to leap from the Republican party to the Democratic—away from my parents' party to one of my own, once more in line with the kind of values and choices I thought Jesus would make. I felt sure Jesus would ordain me if he were a bishop—or still enfleshed.

I was driven by the ongoing sting of the verdict of rejection that the ordination screening committee had imposed: "*2.24-too-many children.*" This meant that I couldn't be a mother *and* a priest. "Dual vocation" they'd called it. No mention of men and fathers, of course. My younger sister Laurie was there to hug me as I wept, simultaneously declaring me an "asshole" for trying over and over. Rejection drove me forward.

In March, 1979, my youngest sister, Jeanie died unexpectedly after surgery for congenital aneurysms in her brain. She was only 34! Her husband and three young children were bereft. Her death precipitated severe asthma in me. There is nothing like not breathing to make one feel like death. I never thought this was divine punishment. I did, however, feel a terror I hadn't known before. On medical advice, I felt pressured to get rid of our cats, possible allergens. They were my daughter Jill's beloved "babies." She was heart-broken. Fear-based choices *never* work well.

Bill Brakeman had bought a window air conditioner. Dick Simeone, now the rector of the parish, stood by—rather sat by, because during the move into the rectory he had dropped a sink on his big toe which was bandaged and elevated. I thought a lot about the biblical Old Testament, not a single word of which was free of anguish, pain, grief, sin, and relational turmoil. God allowed, absorbed, healed and wept over all of it. Sin and mayhem were as omnipresent as divine love no matter what. I chose it all.

WHITEOUT

My choices were made in a racist context. BUT, to be white did not mean an automatic, anemic "whiteout"— nor did it mean I should be "white-ist" as if my skin color gave me omnipotent status. I worked harder than ever for my freedoms because I was female, and because I remembered Carol Lee.

All my choices, my leaps, my fears, shaped me, hurt me, hurt others, helped me grow, helped others grow, and required amends.

ACT FIFTEEN. WORDS COMING ALIVE.

At every time and in every place along this journey special words came to me as gifts. They played peek-a-boo—appearing, disappearing, reappearing.

SCENE FORTY-ONE. POTENTIATION. THE FIRST DAY.

I am an inveterate note-taker—a nerd. But who do people ask when there's uncertainty? Or, what had that professor said again?

On my first day as a student at YDS, I sat poised, pen in hand, spiral notebook open, my arm resting on the little pop-up writing desk in a huge lecture hall full of upturned faces, The professor of Old Testament, a required course for all of us first-year seminarians, had entered, mounted the podium, slapped a swath of notes onto the awaiting lectern, put on his large dark-rimmed glasses, looked down, then up. A hush fell. And then: "In the beginning God . . ."

Potentiated.

But no, it said the earth was void and empty. Empty like a womb? Like deep sorrow? Waiting? Depressed? Like me? I heard a word not spoken.

* * * *

We had been told that we'd be using the Revised Standard Version (RSV), published in 1952. The King James Version (KJV) of the Bible was published in 1611 and remained the most popular for its eloquent, but not very usable, prose. Translations proliferated, evolved, according to *exigencies* of the times. Creation was obviously ongoing!

Who said potentiation? I know I heard it, and fell quickly in thrall to its dramatic potency.

Potentiation?

God-school provided a new context, new words, and in time the presence of new genders. The students were mostly white, male, Protestant, I surmised, because I didn't see a lot of quickie self-blessings with the sign of the cross. I felt *potentiated*.

Later we streamed into the refectory for lunch. I found my "group"—my pod without the peas. We were aging mid-life women in our forties, all white, most of us commuters, some with spouses and children at home, all of different Christian denominations—Lutheran, United Church of Christ, one Catholic, and three Episcopalians. We were chatty and excited about jumping into potentiation, even though I was the only one who heard it.

I headed for my car at dusk to drive home, lugging the biggest, newest brand new Bible I'd ever seen or owned. I felt scared. By the time I got home it was dark. I hugged my children, threw some supper together, and sat down with my notes and my outsized holy text. I could underline all I wanted, which meant practically

ACT FIFTEEN. WORDS COMING ALIVE.

every word. I would study for this potentiation till I dropped. I had craved independence and discovered freedom.

What I began to experience was that God created freedom of choice, not paradise. Biblical people were all mixed up and messed up, yet somehow they kept getting re-potentiated—back in sync with God who, for no sane reason, went on potentiating. Anything could happen. I felt just like these ancients—fascinated and fearful. Risky business this kind of spiritual freedom.

What if I chose wrong, and what if God exiled me, or I rejected God?

Despite some mixed feelings, I dived in—too much, because once when a child came begging for one more cookie, I said: "Leave me alone, I'm reading my Bible." Oh God. I leaped up and gave him TWO cookies.

SCENE FORTY-TWO. INERRANCY

The big required hot-shot basic courses had one lecture and three section meetings a week. To my surprise, Jim Echols, a young black man, a student in the doctoral program, was the teaching assistant of my section in the Old Testament Theology course. I don't know why his black skin color surprised me, but of course a God-school in the *northeast* could never be racially segregated—only sexually.

Jim was tall and lean, with a lavish but neatly trimmed afro. We were invited to call him Jim. I loved his sense of humor, his mild, slightly amused manner, and his willingness to entertain any and all argument. Jim believed in and taught us biblical inerrancy, the idea that there were no errors or faults in the Holy Bible.

Inerrancy?

What? That's nuts! What about God's telling Abraham to kill his son Isaac as proof of Abe's great faith? What about God's having created, even invited, sin in the first place in Genesis? What about God's holy wrath—wholly unjust? I argued ferociously against this inerrancy idea. Jim listened with kindness. I thought he was completely wrong. I mean he was a black man. What about racial injustice in the Bible? How about women? Errant and still holy?

What I noticed as I pored over the Hebrew Scriptures, however, was how easily I assumed that all those biblical people were white-skinned and saintly, Christianized. In story after story God as Creator seemed quite content to include the whole messy array of characters in the divine plan to keep this creation thing going—all of it good. If not, why did God refrain from blasting Eve out of Eden, exile her after her brilliant grab for freedom? And why had Sarah survived divine wrath after laughing at the absurdity of God's promise that she'd get pregnant in old—very old—age? There were countless examples of divine "errancy"—Ruth, Miriam, Hagar, Job's wife who cursed God, Moses the murderer, Samson the flirt who suffered a great wound to his ego after his flirtations, David the adulterer, and more. Sin was in!

Jim stuck with his inerrancy platform while I struggled mightily with my confusion and my effort to make this Holy Bible literal, factual, historical, infallible. I kept going to lectures and listening to Jim anyway. After a time I found consistency. It was God who *never* erred in love. Jim Echols *never* erred in his tolerance of all of us floundering students. He would always tell us to watch for the WHOLE story and let it evolve. There's always a story, he'd say.

ACT FIFTEEN. WORDS COMING ALIVE.

Jim died in 1967. He had pursued his inerrant God and served as the first African American president of a North American Lutheran Seminary and as academic dean at the former Lutheran Theological seminary in Philadelphia. He died December 23 after a fall at his Philadelphia home. I wrote:

Dear Jim,

Thank you, Jim, for not evading all the academic material of scripture, yet always saying: "Remember there is a story here, too." I felt alive. Stories. Stories move. Stories evolve. My story too. I wrote in my little blue final exam book: O.T. LIVES!! You added a big red exclamation point right next to mine. You gave me a new word to ponder: inerrancy. You expanded my little white world, my little Christian world.

*PS. Today in twenty-first century America, there is so much confusion over facts that we're losing the founding vision of our nation. What is a fact and what is fake news? How do we evaluate the news of the day? It seems to depend on who says it. Some call this era post-truth We need leaders like you, Jim, to help us see both facts and truth in context, the larger vision within well-examined, well-articulated facts. We need to remember there's always **an ongoing story.***

By the way, Jim, here's an inerrant truth, obviously not a fact: There are NO white people in the Bible.

With affection and thanks, Lyn Brakeman, addled student of OT at YDS.

SCENE FORTY-THREE. IMMANENCE

This other big word I discovered when I took a course in Systematic Theology. It was full of excellent information about how the Christian Church developed through Councils of bishops and academic scholars, all men of course, who decided what was orthodox for Christians to believe and what was, well, heresy, not a good thing to embrace. In ancient times you could die for heresy.

These Church councils took place in the ancient cities of Nicaea and Chalcedon in the third century. The Nicene Creed we recited every Sunday in the parish church. To me it was totally boring and full of stuff that made me bristle as if I were allergic to repeating *I believe*, or *We believe*, over and over when I didn't really believe it, or all of it.

I did pick up one vital bit of orthodoxy that I loved. At the 451 BC Chalcedon Council, the early Church concluded that Jesus the Christ was BOTH divine and human at once—fully divine AND fully human. Impossibly life-saving, both/and theology for me back then and now.

ACT SIXTEEN.
NEW TESTAMENT

I had hoped for a brand new set of ideas the way I'd yearned for a bright shiny new bike when I hit my teens. That was blissfully immature of course, but surely the NEW testament held promise, especially since I knew that immanence was a very good thing for an introvert to know every day. Also, I needed something new and renewable.

Could Jesus jump out of all those stained glass windows and flesh out?

SCENE FORTY-FOUR. LUKE TIMOTHY JOHNSON AND IMMANENCE THEOLOGY

This New Testament professor was spry—darn near jolly-old-elfish. He promised that something new *and* different would be squeezed out of anything old. The syllabus indicated that we would begin with Mark, written about 50 CE and impressively activist. Every Sunday School thing I'd ingested was about to be dashed on the rocks of scholarship.

The room fell silent. Into that solemn silence someone sneezed—loudly and explosively. Luke Johnson responded without missing a beat: "God bless you and all vegetative processes." Everyone laughed—and breathed. Thus was launched the New Testament.

I was to benefit from Luke Johnson's scholarship as well as his style and his pastoral care. He was totally delighted doing what he was doing—lecturing about holy texts to uninformed and unformed—students, some even middle-aged women like me bucking the tides of sexism!

I made an appointment to talk with him about my fears and frets about the Episcopal Church and my having been turned down in the Connecticut ordination process. I knew Luke was Roman Catholic and had even been a monastic. He too had been hurt by his church when he, in spite of the fact that he was married and had a child, was refused laicization. I was trying to get un-laicized. He wanted out of the ranks and I wanted in.

"I love the Bible and your course, of course," I stammered when we met. Luke nodded. "I am trying to be ordained as a priest in the Episcopal Church, and the resistance to women priests is, well, stiff." (Such a perfect word!) Luke listened to my feelings with care. He was supportive with no answers or judgments.

ACT SIXTEEN. NEW TESTAMENT

As we wrapped up I stood to leave just as another professor walked by Luke's open office door. This professor was an academic type—tall, erect, and fully uniformed in black with the traditional high-rise Anglican clerical collar. He was a nice man, kind and learned, specializing in Patristics (old guys—called Fathers—who articulated early church politics and the theological justifications thereof). We students liked him, while we joked that we bet he slept in his stiff mile-high collar.

Nodding in his direction, Luke said softly with a smile: "Lyn, you don't fit the model." Damn, I had a vagina but no penis! "But God knows who you are, so trust God."

It was another "Carol Lee" moment: I wanted Divinity under my skin—immanent—and it felt as if Divinity/God was out of reach.

I decided to dive into my latest God-word: *Immanence*. Luke Johnson used this word a lot. Immanence tugged at my soul It was close to *imminence* but with much more— ah!—profundity.

One reason I found Immanence so alluring was that it described the God I'd met under the table as a child— intimate, reachable, and silently conversational. Immanent means "remaining within"—available, thumping like my heart. Pulpit descriptors and assumptions about Divinity were about God as transcendent, almighty, conditional, unreachable, and distant. But Jesus's prayers sounded just like mine—intimate, pleading, moaning, mourning, and praising all at once.

SCENE FORTY-FIVE. BILL MUEHL AND IMMANENT PREACHING

As I was rejoicing over Immanence I was simultaneously more and more exposed to people in seminary whose skin was not white like mine. God, I figured, was immanent in them as well as in all critters. I gleaned this from the vast Creation story in Genesis in which all life is shot through and thoroughly permeated by divine artistry. Immanence was the classy theological word for it—a word that made racist and sexist imagery for Creation impossible.

Hearing black students preach with zeal, practically shouting, confirmed for me the impossibility of racism in God's world. Black preaching and worship in the YDS chapel was more like cheerleading than preaching. I loved it. Students prepared written sermons of course, but the moment of truth came with the delivery—out loud from a pulpit/lectern in front of the class with the professor, William (Bill) Muehl, listening and taking notes.

Muehl had a sharp, wry wit, was a lawyer by training, and famous for his book *All The Damned Angels* (1972) in which he deplored all sorts of rigid moralisms and gooey piety about the crucifixion and its bold dominance in Christian parlance. He once said that a miracle could be performed *by accident,* as in while no one was looking. He wrote about Immanence being God's life in *all* flesh: "I have had to be content with damned angels and the facts of life."

ACT SIXTEEN. NEW TESTAMENT

Bill Muehl brought God down to earth and expected the same from us preaching students.

I was already suspicious of too much unfleshly transcendence. I did not adore the painful crucifix as if it were divine, although having to preach to Bill Muehl might feel that scary. I took courage from the black students who did not seem scared as they let their faith in Jesus rip and roar with vigor, energy, and an intimacy I loved and feared. Was I too white? Muehl would bemoan the fact that he never understood how students did well in his preaching classes and then got out there and preached "pap" in their parishes. Was I a future pap-preacher?

The text Muehl assigned for the day I was to be the preacher in class was one of St. Paul's semicolon-rich passages in Romans 5— all about justification by faith through grace via Christ crucified, and then actually bragging about personal sufferings because "suffering produces endurance, and endurance produces character, and character produces hope, and hope does not disappoint us." Why? Because God's love had been *poured* into our hearts by the Holy Spirit.

The word *poured* jumped off the page at me, so I imagined a huge pitcher full of Divinity, somehow liquified or magically de-solidified, pouring into me. I'd never heard of water-boarding, thank heavens, and water seemed safer to me than Christ's blood. This, I figured, was a kind of suffering when I tried, through my sermon, to convey the joyful horror of drowning in God.

I'd already developed a severe case of pulpit-paralysis at a podium for a small class.

Black students had to be just as scared as I was, but when they got in that pulpit their words sang with Immanence, jumped for joy. It was so intimate that listeners talked back: *Preach it sister! Say it! Amen! Yes!*

Was I too white for this, too Episcopalian?

Muehl advised against imitation of black preaching and told me to be myself. "You'll get used to it," he told me, adding something like, "but of course you'll get flack about your female voice, so pitch low." I told him I was an alto. I passed the course.

ACT SEVENTEEN. PRACTICING IMMANENCE

How odd that my frantic search for God would turn out to be my anti-racism training—or part of it anyway.

SCENE FORTY-FIVE. CHRISTIAN EXISTENCE AS LIVING IN THE SPIRIT

I pursued God's identity with foolish yet honest greed as if I could contain, possess, ground, or at least secure Divinity. *"The Spirit searches everything, even the depths of God . . ."* (I Cor. 2:10b). I'd read this in St. Paul's letter to the Corinthians. It became a touchstone—mysteriously impossible to achieve and control in any way, yet always available. No wonder people sang and praised amazing grace so much. It was a recipe. How to get it, and hold onto to it, and keep the supply lines open remained a mystery.

I wrote about Carol Lee and my painful compromise. *"Part of the little-girl-God in me died. Is God black?"*

I remembered a terrifying sledding accident that happened after we had moved to North Canton, Connecticut. Our daughter Jill almost lost her eyesight. I was out of town and my parents were watching out for the children. Jill's sled hit an icy patch going down the slope. Her sled went over the bank and headlong into a barbed wire fence. Screaming and covered with blood, Jill ran back to the house for help, her frightened cousin right with her, calling, "Jill, are you all right?" Jill was not all right. When they got to the house Ether opened the door and sprang into action at the sight. She grabbed Jill up into her strong arms, got towels, and yelled for my father who came running. He drove as fast as he dared to the hospital, and Ether sat in the back seat holding Jill and keeping pressure on her head to stanch the bleeding. Jill later told me: "She held my head so hard against her body, like she was holding me together." At the hospital a brilliant plastic surgeon named Dr. Joan Platt stitched Jill's face up and saved her from blindness.

Ether, a black woman, and Dr. Platt, a white woman, worked together to heal my daughter. I came rushing home and went to the hospital where Jill was in bed all bandaged. Her sight was preserved.

Divinity that day was both black *and* female.

* * * *

Our oldest daughter Bev was sixteen and had just begun driving in 1979 when my sister Jeanie died after surgery for congenital brain aneurysms. Bev often wore large bulky sweatshirts, but when I saw her in a swimsuit she looked emaciated. We found a therapist, and Bev drove herself from Canton to Suffield, Connecticut. I thought she was the bravest young soul I'd ever seen. Later she told me that the therapist "made" her get angry. From Bev I learned courage.

From Jill I soon learned always to tell the truth no matter what. She had told me she felt "second best" to Bev who was only older by a mere 13 months.

ACT SEVENTEEN. PRACTICING IMMANENCE

I also learned what drastic things could happen when the putative divine will was drastically misunderstood and used to justify human ignorance such as racismS.

Being a mother is no more or less holy than anything else, no matter what my mother's "gospel" was. Very slowly I was also realizing that to be black or female was no more or less holy than to be white. But I didn't choose my sex or my skin color. Neither had Carol Lee. And yet God gave us *both* the Spirit of The Holy. A new doxology came my way as I floundered about worrying about God's will and mine colliding.

> The grace of God cannot be fixed
> or fastened to a sanctioned spot;
> when we move as the Spirit moves,
> there is no place where God is not.
> Michael Hudson, text. Doxology/Eighth Tune, 2004.

SCENE FORTY-SIX. SUCH A DEAL!

A child in Church School provided the capstone. The children were reading biblical stories—wondrous tales of woe and weal at once. Noah's Arc is an ancient fable. I was laboring through some explanatory "baloney" about fables when a small boy about six years old lit up. "Oh, so he *branged* them all home!"

Sure enough God *branged* home all the animals, all the children, and even the likes of me.

Exactly what does God in Genesis say about this rainbow? *"When the bow is in the sky I will see it and remember the everlasting covenant between every living creature of all flesh that is on the earth"* (Genesis 9:16).

This Noachean covenant remains a good deal. Watch for rainbows!

SCENE FORTY-SEVEN. WEDDING

On Christ the King Sunday in 1986, the Rev. Richard John Simeone, the rector at my home parish, Trinity, and I married in the midst of a Sunday Eucharist. Our guest list was easy: the congregation and invited family. The setting was unimaginably perfect. At first I'd voiced my aversion to the KING image: "Kings don't work for me!" "Calm down," said Dick. It's Matthew's agenda. You have no idea how many agendas—all of them holy— are faithfully written in Scripture.

I could live with the King idea being Christ, but I unexpectedly wept right in the middle of saying my vows. My therapist stood behind me, rubbing courage into my back, while poor Dick's mustache quivered. I knew this love was completely whole and real. As they say, it was to cry for. God must've *branged* us together.

I wept—not from feelings of failure or regret, but from the sorrow that accompanies a truth too deep to define: The human heart is a spacious vessel, capable of holding many loves and many pains, an infinity of feelings. The divine heart is even more spacious.

ACT EIGHTEEN. LEARNING WITHOUT STUDYING.

When I started to write about my racisms I realized that what moved me was derived from many pressing scenarios, not measurably relevant to racism, or any skin color, but steadily building inside me as a spirituality of deep appreciation for the sheer elegance of every living thing.

SCENE FORTY-EIGHT. EFM

A new way to learn came my way through a woman who was a mentor in the Education for Ministry (EfM) program—spiritual formation as a process of **experiential** learning not enslaved by the academy or the classroom, or even one single faith. No teachy/preachy allowed. There was reading—the whole bible and beyond. Learning was expansive— in small groups, guided by trained mentors, meeting weekly, in person or online, with a schedule each group managed on its own.

I'd never contemplated in a group how Abraham *FELT,* or Eve in the garden, or Bathsheba who got raped, or Jesus who was betrayed, or Judas the betrayer, or MLK, Jr., a hero to his race AND to all of us who seek justice. Where IS divine presence?

The goal of such theological formation is to form and inform Christian lay ministry, especially about Scripture, Church History, Spirituality, and Ministry. It is not doctrinal or dogmatic. It is discernment through theological reflection, a process that uses metaphors, not lectures, to illuminate difficult issues. My favorite image for the whole EfM process is the Yin-yang of ALL creation. It freed me to develop and fly. Dick and I also trained to be diocesan coordinators for EfM in the Diocese of Massachusetts.

SCENE FORTY-NINE. LESSONS ON DYING FROM THE DYING

From the sick-unto-death I learned not to fear death.

After seminary my mind had felt swollen to the point of explosion, yet equally drained of energy. I felt full as if I'd overeaten. I couldn't learn one single additional thing, pray one more prayer for me to get ordained. Even my already wheezing lungs couldn't inhale one more breath—for the Lord or anyone. And my eyes wept dry tears.

Nevertheless, there was one more requirement—one more torturous shredding of my ego I feared. They called it Clinical Pastoral Education, CPE for short. I would be trained to work in a hospital, to give solace, comfort, and spiritual hope to the sick and the dying. I had little to give, except listening with care.

My God, how I wished I could just hop into one of those beds with the crisp white taut sheets, push the button to summon a kindly

ACT EIGHTEEN. LEARNING WITHOUT STUDYING.

nurse to wash my feet or offer sweet oblivion with some pain killer drug. No one *learns* humility, it is given like grace.

I was a hospital chaplain, supervised at UConn Health Center by a Roman Catholic nun, later in a group of trainees at Hartford Hospital. Chaplaincy work opened my soul.

* * * *

I stood with a family at the bedside of their dying child. They had three daughters, all with muscular dystrophy—a wasting disease with, no cure. The oldest had died; the middle daughter lay dying; the youngest, maybe 7 or 8, sat in a wheelchair next to her sister's bed, her face twisted in agony. A machine whooshed, sucked, and sighed as it pumped last-minute breaths into the dying child's lungs.

The family had seen this before. The nurses had summoned me, a small female plainclothes chaplain, alongside a Roman priest, a robust specimen as well done and rounded as a pot roast. He brandished healing oils and stood close to the child in the wheelchair, muttering too many prayers. The rest of us surrounded the bed with powerless presence. I thought I should say something, but nothing occurred to me, so I stood silently by. The priest looked down upon the now sobbing child in the wheelchair and said, "Oh now, don't cry. Aren't you happy your sister will soon be with the angels in heaven?" The child turned her small tear-stained face upward and countered him with fierce rage: "NO. NO. I don't care about angels. I want my sister!"

This was the most honest prayer I'd ever heard. I knew that God wept with us all as we watched the nurse unplug respirator and listened as the dying girl's breaths space out slowly, slowly, and then stop.

* * * *

On another occasion, a dying man in his seventies, taught me theology. The man knew his death was close. We'd talked about it, and he was as ready to die as anyone ever is. I was not ready for him to die. He told me he'd prayed a lot that God would change things, but he also seemed peaceful with the truth, and thought it must be God's will. I, however, had come to know and care about this man, and uttered the following stunningly unprofessional spontaneous idiocy: "We pray, believing that God saves, heals, and all this, but why would such a great big almighty God bother?"

"Why wouldn't he?" the man said.

SCENE FIFTY. LESSONS FROM BLACKS ON BEING BLACK

O.T. was in my Hartford Hospital chaplaincy group. He was the most contagiously jolly man I'd ever met. I don't know how he did it, but O.T. could laugh—always. Compassionate humor was his greatest pastoral gift. He offered what I called kindness laughter—essential when one of us trainees felt helpless, or had just uttered something utterly real but pastorally clumsy.

Once one of us was making a pre-surgery visit to a patient who said he was having his lung removed, and before he could explain about transplant, this chaplain, pale with horror, blurted: "The whole thing?" This chaplain was consumed with guilt about his blunder, and O.T. said: "Don't fret, honey, they remove it in halves." O.T even found honest humor in death? From him I learned, again and more forcefully, that God was not the ultimate "almighty" dour potentate we'd been taught to revere and fear, but that God gave us laughter alongside tears. How else does one cope in this ministry?

When O.T landed his first job at a big Baptist church in Newark, he invited Dick to deliver the pastoral charge, that is, a pep talk addressed to the newly ordained minister about how to manage a first official ministry, chiefly, follow the teachings of Jesus, and try

ACT EIGHTEEN. LEARNING WITHOUT STUDYING.

not to get fired before you burn out. Dick accepted O.T.'s invitation with fervor and fear. O.T said: "Just say it, brother." Dick hit the pulpit running. Neither of us remembers what he said, but it passed muster. A white preacher in a black church receiving enthusiastic talk-back felt like a just-right miracle.

* * * *

From Alice Walker, a black woman author I learned about prayer and female sass. In her 1982 book, *The Color Purple*, she wrote in the voice of her main character Celie:

"I think it pisses God off if you walk by the color purple in a field somewhere and don't notice it. People think pleasing God is all God cares about. But any fool living in the world can see it always trying to please us back."

Celie continues: " . . . *have you ever found God in church? I never did. I just found a bunch of folks hoping for him to show. Any God I ever felt in church I brought in with me. And I think all the other folks did too. They come to church to share God, not find God."*
"I think us here to wonder, myself. To wonder."

* * * *

So far I was getting my anti-racism training from biblical text, academic theology, the dying, black ministers, secular feminism, exquisitely honest black writers, and my own emotionally-charged spirituality.

SCENE FIFTY-ONE. LESSONS FROM ALKIES
ON SOBRIETY

I now needed a job with money. I looked in the want ads under "C" for church. Now, how many churches advertise in this way? Lo! There was an ad for a Chaplain. I knew how to do this ministry, and

I wanted a setting less, well, full of certain death. I applied for the chaplaincy job at a newly opened treatment center for alcoholics.

I knew a lot about drinking but not much about not drinking. I got the job in part because the Director who interviewed me liked my "grounded" spirituality. She'd been afraid I'd come in swinging Jesus around like a lethal baseball bat. I told her my Jesus was down-to-earth—had dirt under his fingernails. She laughed and hired me.

I served as chaplain at BlueRidge Alcohol and Drug Treatment Center from 1984 to1990 when it closed for lack of funds. After I was ordained deacon in 1987, I wore my clerical collar to work one day and everyone cheered.

I learned more from those alkies and druggies than I ever thought possible. I learned that fear bred loneliness, and that shame murdered the soul. We human critters simply must speak and *listen* to each other and to ourselves.

The principles of the Twelve Steps to Recovery were a lot like my religious faith or the spirituality thereof: you just had to let go of control to gain self-control. That sounded laughably impossible. All it meant was that you had to stop trying to control everything under the sun and open up to the culturally UNpopular idea: "I can't do it myself." This wisdom did not mean you were a helpless wimp. It simply meant that you needed other people and God/ Higher Power, to lend a hand all along the entire way of life—hope, courage, trust, compassion, and silent presence in the dark.

These alkies were stubborn as hell, funnier than any comedian, resent-full, and paralyzed by a toxic shame too fierce to mention and more life-threatening than the worst of intoxicants.

Once a very big black man sat listening to my talk on spirituality. He rose up to let me know that everything I said was full of shit. I

ACT EIGHTEEN. LEARNING WITHOUT STUDYING.

shot back: "Sit down and shut up, sir. I've listened to all your shit, and now you have to listen to mine."

ACT NINETEEN. HOW HOLY IS HOLY?

This is a question I used to ask a lot, as if there were degrees or gradations of holiness. Could HOLY dwell alongside sin?

SCENE FIFTY-TWO. SEX HOLY?

Rudolph Otto had defined the contradictory power of the Holy as *mysterium tremendum et fascinans.* One could be overwhelmed or afraid of something or someone, and at the very same time be fascinated and drawn to it.

I knew Divinity was obviously not white or male, because I was female, and Jesus was semitic. I explored the Holy in many guises: Jewish? Christian? Episcopalian? Gay? Womb? Tomb? Male? Female? Father? Mother? Transcendent? Immanent? Almighty? Angry? Judge? Lover? Sexual? Asexual? Socialist? Capitalist? Communist? Whatever the Holy was it continued to be elusive and alluring at once.

In my journal for a course called "Christian Existence as Life in the Spirit" I had written about being sexually molested at age eight in a New York City theater by an old man who looked like every image I'd ever seen of God. I wrote: "*Terror is breathless. I am paralyzed.*

ACT NINETEEN. HOW HOLY IS HOLY?

Then I feel a hot dimly pleasurable sensation as his finger probes. Why don't I move? I can't. I am trapped in a net, caught between the repulsion of molestation and the attraction of clitoral sensations, and the message: never tell. I think something is wrong with me. It's my fault." Was this experience tremendum et fascinans?

Is sex Holy? Could holy matrimony be a harness? I wrote: "*A sexual relationship is of God and flies free like the Gospel. Can sexual behavior be a matter of duty, mechanical, rigid, conforming, conscripting? One message said: you are beautiful, and sexually responsive, and a woman. The other said: you are a dutiful and sexually performing wife. Ghosting these two was childbirth and mothering.*

For me, there was nothing more holy than birthing and rearing a child. The exertion of birthing felt like God creating. Birthing, nursing, chasing, crawling, hugging, observing, forbidding, letting go, hanging on, listening—all of it holy. It feels like balancing on a tightrope as children grow—exhausting and miraculous at once. Yet, maternal love never abates; it just gets roomier, and very likely more helpless.

What is *fascinating* is that maternal love is imperfect yet always growing. What is *tremendously mysterious* is how much forgiving goes on—self-forgiving, forgiving between mother and child, and divine forgivingness for countless blunders everywhere in everyone.

All kinds of so-called "immoral" behavior felt holy to me—affairs, masturbation, divorce, sin— all of it sacred power, none of it shaped or confined by traditional morality. At midlife I was getting sick of functioning like a metronome, tick-tocking my way along the path of prescribed "shoulds." The professor commented in my journal's margins that my search reminded him of D.H Lawrence's *Lady Chatterly's Lover* wherein "sexual energy so long blocked and finally released was seen as sacred power."

SCENE FIFTY-THREE. ANGER HOLY?

After the Episcopal Church turned me down in the ordination process, I'd felt the pain of shame AND, strangely, the liberating energy of fury. *Tremendum et fascinans.*

Most of what I'd learned about anger was that it was *bad*, made trouble, and was unbecoming for women—as in hell hath no fury like hers.

Anger is damned hard to express without hurting or being hurt, and double-damned hard to feel without a target (self or other) to blame. Nothing serene here. But boy, does anger released and relieve stored-up stagnating energy, like a bull confined in a rodeo stall just before the gate swings open. The bull was handicapped by the unjust rules that used his natural rage against him. So was I in this game called patriarchy.

SCENE FIFTY-FOUR. MONEY HOLY? ORDAINED SO.

What about MONEY or material WEALTH? Only shared does it have value. Poverty, I realized, was/is a death-dealing social disease—tragically and unjustly racialized AND gendered, not to mention institutionalized.

* * * *

While I'd waited for my Church's imprimatur, I took courses at the UConn School of Social Work where I discovered the work of Antonio Gramsci (1891-1937). Gramsci, himself a member of the ruling class (moneyed) taught that the ruling moneyed class used established cultural institutions to reinforce norms and values that maintained their own hegemony, hence capitalism dominated and domineered. Money ruled. *Tremendum.*

ACT NINETEEN. HOW HOLY IS HOLY?

Gramsci, a neo-Marxist, critiqued materialism and advocated a more humanistic understanding of Marxism. He even helped to organize the working classes. *Fascinans.*

What I took from this class was the idea that Gramsci was in favor of a capitalist economy *and* a socialist society. I didn't like Communism or Socialism much, but thought socialist values could empower true Democracy and protect the right of every citizen of age to vote. Such equity could make a huge dent in CapitalISM and in *all* my "racismS."

Jesus would certainly be a socialist, I thought. He despised wealthism, and was clearly against any kind of social or economic injustice—any and all -isms. He, and the Divinity he proclaimed, were obviously not in favor of taxing the poor while the rich, by all means of unholy practices, got richer. However, Jesus himself did *not* live in poverty, for if he had, he would never have had the energy to walk the rough terrain of the land, teach, preach, heal, weep, forgive, and pray. He had help from friends.

* * * *

My own prescription: keep praying like crazy, continue paid chaplaincy work and pastoral counseling work, try masturbation, get married for love and sex, love your children honestly and imperfectly, get a woman therapist, grieve, go on spiritual/prayer retreats, have a spiritual director, read radical stuff, keep old friends, and get political.

* * * *

The Episcopal Church in Connecticut, would soon elect a new bishop. Would he (of course) look with favor on this well-tested thoroughly anti-racist aspirant?

He did, with a little help from a female priest I had lobbied. I was ordained deacon in 1987 and priest in 1988 by the Rt. Rev. Arthur E. Walmsley.

ACT TWENTY. ONGOING/ REMEMBERED FORMATION

I had discovered that personal independence comes with courage and creativity and grit, *also* failure and education and experimentation—plus sweet accidentally perceived god-moments. Independence, like freedom, comes when you rely on yourself AND the help of many others, keep faith in Divinity by whatever name—*never* by waging violent wars.

SCENE FIFTY-FIVE. SPIRITUAL DIRECTIONS

I'd first met Pierre Wolff, S.J. at Mercy Center in Madison, Connecticut where he met with people for Spiritual Direction. He was very French, very radical, and very popular. He did not like the way his Roman Catholic church treated women. I didn't like the way *any* church treated women.

I trusted Pierre and began to see him regularly at his home in Wallingford, CT. He guided me through the Spiritual Exercises of St. Ignatius of Loyola and beyond. The experience of, dare I say, getting to know Jesus as a man of flesh with true feelings, even anger, was intense—more real than any sermons I'd ever heard.

I also trusted Mercy sisters anywhere yet chiefly at Mercy Center in Madison, Connecticut. I became an Associate of Mercy—mercifully short of becoming a vowed sister, yet rich in spiritual potentiation, including much laughter and silent prayer retreats during which I made a lot of noise—prayerfully of course.

Most Christians dehumanize the Incarnate Lord—too holy for words. Pierre and the Mercies helped me weep and rage as Jesus did. The crucified Jesus to me will never be an image of anything but cruel politics, profound injustice, and hatred. This was not, is not, nor ever shall be, the will of God/Creator whose Love is deep enough to respect and redeem freedom. Crazy Holy, right?

In time, Pierre left his Roman church. His orders were received in the Episcopal Church, meaning he did not have to be RE-ordained. I officiated at his marriage to Sister Mary Morgan. She will always be a Mercy, not living in community. Pierre will always be a Jesuit—my Jesuit. So far they haven't "de-jesuitized" him.

SCENE FIFTY-SIX. MADELEINE L'ENGLE

It started, as most good things do, when inner desire meets outer teacher. For me that teacher was author Madeleine L'Engle from whom I had learned how to be a truthful "snake" (see scene 32)

Other stories followed the snake, each one about a biblical woman making her case for justice and clarity before God/Creator. Together these stories, all conversations with God, became my first book, *Spiritual Lemons, Biblical Women, Irreverent Laughter and Righteous Rage*, first published by Luramedia in 1997, and continues in print with Augsburg Fortress and Wipf and Stock.

The most difficult story to write was the one about Mary the mother of Jesus, who argued with God, "This is MY son!" At one of my readings, a Roman Catholic woman protested that I was not honoring Mother Mary who had willingly offered her son up. After

ACT TWENTY. ONGOING/REMEMBERED FORMATION

the reading this same woman came up to me with tears in her eyes: "My daughter wants to become a nun and I don't want her to." She sobbed. We hugged. I learned again that there is *always* a story ready to stretch to unfurl deep emotional truth.

ACT TWENTY-ONE.
INDEPENDENCE FOR WHOM?

Historically, "Independence" meant America's Declaration of Independence—her freedom from British rule. Well, okay, and we wealthy whities have not lived out our precious independence in equitable ways, now have we? We could call it *white* independence, or *wealthy white* independence or *wealthy white male* independence.

BUT IT'S NOT, RIGHT?

SCENE FIFTY-SEVEN. READING RITA

I read the autobiographical novel *Rubyfruit Jungle* by Rita Mae Brown, published in 1973. Brown was born in 1944 to an unwed teenage mother who left her at an orphanage from which a cousin of her mother rescued her and raised her in Pennsylvania and Florida.

Rita Mae Brown hitchhiked to New York City in the 1960s and got advanced degrees in Classics and English at NYU. Brown was also a writer who used her gift, not as a political act, but rather to eschew the label of "lesbian." Labeling—a very common but ungodly

ACT TWENTY-ONE. INDEPENDENCE FOR WHOM?

practice—confines and defines and separates. This includes all our many labels that constrict and define DIVINITY.

When I read *Rubyfruit Jungle* I was initially amazed at such transparent candor, then wowed by the sex a woman could experience—all by herself if she so desired or even with another woman. I tried it all, and WOW. Masturbation and a sexual experience with a lesbian seminarian friend awakened me to my own sexual power—not simply to "fight" for feminist causes or to procreate, but to relish and cherish my own body—to its fullest and for its own sake. It also taught me never to condemn the sexual preferences of others. HeterosexISM joined my "racismS" list. It includes all our labels for Divinity/ Creator of all.

SCENE FIFTY-EIGHT. TONI

I got to know Toni Morrison, née Chloe Ardelia Wofford in 1931, in Lorain, Ohio, through reading her novel *Beloved* published in 1988, the year I was ordained priest.

Morrison converted to Roman Catholicism at age 12, the age I was when my parents had moved me out of my city into a suburb. I too had dabbled in Roman Catholicism, seeing the sacramental liturgy as embodied, mystical, and a way to get the "Holy" to touch down, or at least be contained between the covers of books. It helped that the Mass was in Latin.

Tony Morrison added Anthony, hence Toni, to her name, choosing St. Anthony of Padua as her baptismal name. "Toni" of Padua (1195-1231) was a Portuguese Catholic priest and Franciscan friar, noted for his knowledge of scripture, powerful preaching, and devotion to the poor and the sick. He is the patron saint of lost things, including causes and respect.

This saint of Padua was a nerd who studied and read and wrote a lot. So did Toni Morrison. So did I. Words—soul motors—fueled my life engine and formed my anti-racist spirituality.

When Morrison was young she had an argument with a little black girl about whether there was a real God or not. She wrote: *"I said there was, and she said there wasn't and she had proof: she had prayed for, and not been given, blue eyes. I just remember listening to her and imagining her with blue eyes, and it was a grotesque thing. She had these high cheek bones and these great big slanted dark eyes, and all I remember thinking was that if she had blue eyes she would be horrible."* (Anecdote taken from Hilton Als July 27, 2020, *New Yorker* profile of Morrison, "Ghosts in the House.")

In and through reading Morrison's writing I felt liberated—also frightened. The energy that surged through her words and characters flew into me like a sharp arrow piercing my soul—not for murder but for joy. Morrison's language itself set me on fire. Of course God knew better than to give this black child blue eyes, right?

* * * *

Morrison's book, *Beloved,* is about a runaway slave who murders her child rather than allow it to be captured and enslaved. It chilled me to the bone and stung me with the memory of Carol Lee and my own first racist decision as a teen. Did God we called Father murder the one we called Son? For a second, my emotions shot back to how I felt when my own parents moved me away from my beloved city. I thought they were racist. Later I wondered if their decision had also freed me to know and love my own white flesh as it was, also to understand that others could do the same in the flesh they were given?

ACT TWENTY-TWO.
EMBODIMENTS

Even after I was ordained, given authority by male bishops to preach from pulpits and preside at altars, I did *not look* the part. I was/am a very short, small-bodied white woman with a stole that nearly touched the floor—also divorced, remarried, rejected twice (almost thrice) in the ordination process, and marked with a questionable reputation, which, by the way, happens to *anyone* who tries to create justice *before* it is legislated and fully accepted.

Prey pray.

Parish pews were filled with white people only. Most wardens, managers of parish functioning and money, were male. Women, called The Altar Guild, set the table, cleared it after everyone had been served and eaten their fill.

These ladies, full of delicate duty and buried rage, set and reset until the next meal.

SCENE FIFTY-EIGHT. SO WHO *IS* THIS BODY OF CHRIST ANYWAY?

I had learned in the Christian and biblical tradition that Jesus the Christ was the bread of life. We had been told that when we consumed this bread—all cleaned up and holy, stacked neatly in wafer piles, not quite resembling its part either, we joined body and soul into the Body of Christ.

I could not forget, however, that buried deep within that "bread" were the tears of women, ancient and modern over the centuries, women who sweated and bled to provide and survive in cultures of patriarchal oppression. Oppression was sometimes canonical, sometimes violent, and sometimes subtle, but one way or another women were ruled out, left out, kept out, held down while their bodies were often used for male pleasure, OR to breed sons only, heirs to divine thrones somewhere. If son, good. If daughter, disposable—except of course to bake more bread, set things up for men to consume and consecrate and call the Body of Christ.

I recited to myself all the familiar pushbacks contemporary women offered: we've come so far, things have changed a lot, stop whining and be patient. Yes, yes, yes, and so what? The Body of Christ is not whole until The Body Politic is also whole—not the same but whole.

* * * *

In parish churches on All Saints' Day we hear a biblical reading from Ecclesiasticus, the Wisdom of Sirach. I dreaded it every year. Why do we have to read this? I'd asked the priest in my first parish, my first parish supervisor. He, very strangely, was black, really brown or mixed black, yet I was sure he would understand my discomfort.

It's assigned, he said.

ACT TWENTY-TWO. EMBODIMENTS

But it's in the apocryphal section, I protested.

Apocryphal literature is canonical in our tradition, he reminded me.

And so AGAIN I'd listened to this "wise" passage, read by a tall man with a loud voice, who began in sonorous, majestic tones.

"Let us now praise famous men."

On and on it rambled. My cheeks shuddered keeping back a yawn. Of course Israel should praise its noble ancestors, those responsible for their survival and their liberation. Everyone does that. Still, I listened carefully to the list, straining, against all reason, to see if there were any women's names listed. Noah, totally righteous of course. (Did his wife clean up all that animal dung?) Abraham, likewise. Sons, Isaac, and Jacob—patriarchs. The list built to an almighty climax with the amazing Moses. Not yet finished, the list moved onward to Aaron, Moses's brother, who got ordained, no less. It climaxed with the great David, king, savior, and adulterer. The passage was literally true to its opening intention: there are *no* women on this praise list, not to mention that all these men were of course Jewish, as was Jesus.

In my own mind I created my own list—a new list of INfamous women without whom there would be no famous men. My list included contemporary writers such as Isabel Wilkerson, author of the 2010 memoir, *The Warmth of Many Suns: The Epic Story of America's Great Migration.* I heard a reading from Wilkerson's powerful book, so tenderly and respectfully detailing her own parents' courage as they moved north, seeking freedom.

I wouldn't migrate across great expanses of land, yet I also would never forget Carol Lee and never casually say, "My best friend was black"—as if that assertion proved anything. One of my best friends really *was* black. It was the quality of that hearty friendship, even with my shame attached, that was the plumb line against which I measured, my *felt* racism.

Google-magic turned up an obituary that looked like my Carol Lee. She had lived in Quogue, Long Island all her life, married and worked as a nurse. This wisp of proof, plus my emotionally intelligent memory was enough to structure the grid for my writing a book called *Whiteout*.

All I needed were more "infamous" women of courage to make me more "infamous."

SCENE FIFTY-NINE. INFAMY ONGOING. HOLY. LIBERATING.

How does a woman of ill repute, whether justified or not, get her share of the limelight should she so desire, or deserve? Sometimes, maybe often, a woman falls into something *infamous* along the way as she seeks to break free, to breathe free, to let loose the fullness of her own body and soul. Sometimes she has to explode, lest she implode and suffocate. And sometimes infamy liberates justice and equality for everyone.

Infamous means notorious, scandalous, shocking, disreputable, according to the standards of expected or acceptable behavior of the times. A woman might carry the *infamy* label no matter what, and even if it wasn't true. I call this The Magdalene Syndrome.

Mary of Magdala was a biblical woman, much maligned for being a sexual sinner par excellence. Why? She was plagued by seven demons. SEVEN. Who knows why? She might have had multiple personality disorder? Jesus exorcised all seven "demons" with a sweep of his healing hand. He did NOT convert her, he healed her. She therefore became famously known as a repentant sinner.

ACT TWENTY-TWO. EMBODIMENTS

Today we know mental illness is not a sin. NEVERTHELESS, some Pope 300 years later labeled Magdalene a prostitute. Where is that written? Oh, perhaps the men knew something about this female-only sin? God knows they grabbed it whenever they could. BUT this information is NOT stated in Holy Scriptures. Magdalene's apparent "demons" are only referenced in Luke's gospel. The first written gospel, Mark's, never mentions them at all.

Given today's wisdom from modern science and medicine about the effects of trauma, these putative "demons" could today be easily understood in terms of psychiatric symptoms—that is IF there were any symptoms. Rumor carries much weight, both then and now.

What the New Testament text tells us is that Mary Magdalene was a faithful follower of Jesus for most of her days. Maybe she was in love with him. She is the only follower privileged with a vision of Jesus in a semi-resurrected, ascending state, and the only one to whom a direct apostolic commission is given: *Go, Mary, and tell the men what you have seen.* (They won't believe you, but never stop saying it, anyway.) She never did stop, and many women through history continued in her footsteps. Me too! Mary Magdalene is usually pictured in icons as holding an egg, symbol of fertility.

Sadly still, this apostle, Mary Magdalene, canonized as a saint, gets stuck with the sexual sinner label? Religion can be slow to forgive while preaching lavishly about its godliness. But then we've always needed *scapegoats* to insure our own power.

The Snake in Genesis This little snake was scapegoated, shamed over centuries, as being the cause or instigator of the whole messy affair we call THE FALL, meaning the falling away from the loving ways of God and into SIN. Could a snake, or anyone who told the truth no one wanted to hear, become a *cosmic scapegoat*? All the snake said was: you won't die if you eat the forbidden fruit. True, but you may be shamed for the rest of your life—just for falling victims to the sin of patriarchal sexism.

The snake is infamous to this day. Ever wonder why so many women are afraid of snakes? I know the story is "just a story." I know snakes don't talk. BUT, read any children's book for wisdom from ALL voices, including those of animals. This snake poses a powerful spiritual question: Is there grace for the snake? Read her soul-story in *Spiritual Lemons. Biblical Women, Irreverent Laughter and Righteous,* by Lyn G. Brakeman, 1997.

Mary and Martha of Bethany These two exceptional biblical women share July 29th as their saints' day on church calendars. They are portrayed as having been very close friends to Jesus, providing him hospitality many times in his itinerancy. Jesus proclaimed the good news of divine presence NOW in our midst. There has been of course much speculation about these two "sisters" and their gender identity, but I will take the Bible story as it is: a story about two sisters, both equally important to the furtherance of the Gospel.

Martha, the one who cleaned and prepared meals and kept the domestic scene well managed, was ALSO the first woman in the New Testament to declare after the raising of Lazarus that Jesus was the Messiah, the Christ of God incarnate.

Mary was a contemplative type. She listened to Jesus's words with full attention when he offered contemplative retreats at their house in Bethany. Few listened in the deep way that Mary did. Few listen today.

Occasionally I preached dialogue sermons in which the congregation was invited to share their views on a biblical story. There were no "wrong" views. With the Mary/Martha gospel the women in the parish congregation went wild with their own takes and their

ACT TWENTY-TWO. EMBODIMENTS

own emotions. Men too joined in. I just closed with a blessing on ALL our experiences.

Infamous women? Me too. My list grows.

SCENE SIXTY. PASSIVE AGGRESSION LAID BARE

After his sermon, the priest at my *first* parish made an announcement: ME. He introduced me. A small inaudible ripple of awe—not the holy kind—went through the congregation. I stood to take my humble bow. It was obvious to me that these dear people had no idea that I was suddenly going to be one of the clergy on staff as a Sunday regular in their parish. I felt like a "jill-in-the-box" pop-up priest.

The very next Sunday this same priest made another spectacular announcement—this one even worse. He announced that he was going to take some time off—four to six weeks—for a vacation and surgery for his lung cancer. "Lyn will be in charge while I am gone," he concluded and signaled the organist to begin the final hymn.

Passive aggression means that someone, often unable to get in touch with her/his own anger or fear, does something to upset other lives and manages to come off looking innocent. Recipients of such behavior are left feeling enraged and powerless. This time it meant me. I already had a job at a counseling center, and was mother to growing children. Now I was left in charge of a parish congregation, that itself was left in the lurch with the first woman priest they had ever experienced in the flesh.

At least we had each other and we were all in the same boat. We did not drown. We learned how to cultivate compassion—together.

SCENE SIXTY-ONE EARRINGS. ALTAR GUILD. MARINE.

After airing my fury with my beloved spouse who listened and got angry with/for me, I headed out the next Sunday. For no reason except maybe fear, I looked into the suggestions box. It was old and full of cobwebs, but LO! there was a small piece of paper. I picked it out and opened it to read: *The priest should not wear dangling earrings.* I laughed which helped me release some of my smoldering anger. I put it on the rector's desk in an envelope with a message that read: "This note must be for you."

The Altar Guild became my "saviors." The head of it was a lovely white-haired woman who was obviously a very efficient long-term Episcopalian. On my first Sunday alone she put her hand on my shoulder and said: "You didn't know this was going to happen, did you, my dear?" I practically wept for joy. She continued, "Don't worry, dear, we are all here together, and we will help you with anything you need." There wasn't a hint of condescension in her tone. I would be all right.

I served that parish well for nearly two years.

A man named Pete approached me at the farewell coffee hour. I was wary of Pete, because he had refused to receive the bread and wine from me until my last Sunday at that parish when he came to the altar rail, knelt, and opened his hands to receive the wafer from me and drink from the chalice I held to his lips. At the coffee hour after church, Pete, a man of few words and a former military man—Marine—came up to me and said: "Well, you've converted me." We hugged as I thanked him.

Never had the Body of Christ felt so real to me. I knew I was a priest—and a woman.

Is this slow conversionary process not the way deeply rooted traditions learn to breathe?

ACT TWENTY-THREE.
SAINTS/SINNERS?

Both/and.

Saints are prophets of transformation. They come from all over, recognized by their words and deeds, not just from any one religious tradition. Saints and sinners live together, inside us and outside us and from all over the globe. Sainthood is not a moral category, nor a denominational, religious one. People just recognize it. When I get an opportunity to speak with children about saints I just hold a mirror up to them all. They giggle.

SCENE SIXTY-TWO. MARY VIRGIN, MOTHER, THEOTOKOS (God-bearer)

One of the most famous and ill-reputed female heroes/saints of the biblical and church tradition is Mary, the mother of Jesus. She has many names, most of them honorific. AND Mary was a real woman, a young woman who "miraculously" found herself with child, aka pregnant, while she was "betrothed"— engaged, not yet wed. She didn't lie about it, but listened to God's voice guiding her from within. I bet that divine immanence communicated something like: Don't worry, take good care of yourself and the child, and I'll work on Joseph and the Church.

The Roman Church, in its embarrassment about such scriptural transparency, elevated Mary to a place of great esteem, restored her virginity, blessed her forever, *also* virtually eliminated any masculine role in both conception AND parenting—unless you want to put faith in God as both sperm donor AND Heavenly Father forever. Kudos to the Church, Holy Roman no less, for elevating this Mary.

Notice, however, how patriarchal religious politics over time accomplished and set in cement the following policies, disproportionately constraining women:

- impugned the female body as a conception machine
- settled on Mary Magdalene as the omni-scapegoat, creating *The Magdalene Syndrome,* the ugly, unjust brush with which many women are tarred—some innocent, some errant, all forgiven by Divinity.
- enslaved sexual activity within marriage
- put celibacy on a moral high holy ground
- made marriage a sacrament, not of blessing but of control
- outlawed divorce, birth control and abortion, further imprisoning women
- contributed to poverty, overpopulation, sex-trafficking, despair, and crime
- made sure Divinity was advertised as transcendent, almighty, and masculine
- locked the image of God into parenting titles

The Roman Church, by its exclusionary sexist policies, guaranteed the advent and rise of feminISM. Women today, and historically, including my own grandmothers, were my personal models for feminism. One chose college before marriage, and one chose elopement to marry a Jew. I long for the day when the church will let Virgin Mary step off her pedestal, relinquish her virginal holiness, and preach her own Magnificat to churches and seminaries.

ACT TWENTY-THREE. SAINTS/SINNERS?

Saints, named and unnamed, come in all sorts and conditions of people.

SCENE SIXTY-THREE. MY GRANDMOTHERS

Eleanor Sampson Gillespie, my paternal grandmother whom I called Grahmmy, gave up her aspirations to be an opera singer in order to get married and have children. She boasted long and often about being one of the first women in her family to graduate from college, in this case Vassar, class of "aughty-aught" (that's 1900!) She fulfilled her "assigned" vocation well with six children, four sons and two daughters, all of whom called her Ma. My dad, Scottishly named McDonald, was #5, sandwiched, not always comfortably, between two sisters. Ma was an imposing presence, pigeon-chested like any proper diva would be. She had a beautiful singing voice, and most evenings after dinner she would assemble her "boys" around the piano to sing. She sang along with gusto. A family "opera."

Marguerite Gordon Hall Adams, my maternal grandmother whom I called Ga, and occasionally Goggie or Gagarrhea if I was miffed, defied her family and eloped with her beloved when she was eighteen. Ga grew up in Medford Massachusetts. She was born into a well-to-do family and lived in a large house, let's say, small mansion. She met and fell in love with a man of Jewish (Ashkenazi) heritage by the name of Avon Franklin Adams, an impresario who imported musical talent from Europe to this country, in particular to New York City, quite bereft in the 1920s of classical musicians. He brought concert violinist Jascha Heifitz and Alma Gluck, to name just two, to this country. Both artists were Jewish.

A.F. Adams's Jewish identity horrified the Hall family. So the young couple eloped! They were married in Manhattan at the non-denominational Church of the Strangers, established in 1868 by the Rev. Charles Alexander Force Deems. He was a Methodist elder who moved to New York City from North Carolina to pastor the Church of the Strangers on January 1, 1891.

I can't tell you how exciting my research process was. To establish my grandfather's Jewishness, and therefore my own, felt redemptive. He died when my mother was just twelve. She was the youngest child of four, born in 1912 when her mother was forty-five. Mom was also her father's favorite. It was apparently mutual, yet Mom held secret his Jewishness for reasons of her own at which I could only guess. I wish I could have met "Pop" Adams as he was called by business colleagues, all grateful for what he did for the classical music scene in America. I remain proud of my heritage *and* my love of classical music.

SCENE SIXTY-FOUR. MY FIRST PATIENT IN ADDICTION REHABILITATION

My experience in parish ministry was, frankly, exhausting. I had trained, loved, and worked in chaplaincy ministry in two general hospitals and one drug/alcohol rehabilitation hospital in Connecticut. To be a chaplain/pastoral presence is a gift I try to give wherever I am. It is the gift of accurate listening with minimal feedback.

Chaplaincy is a more expansive ministry than parish ministry. A chaplain does not have to comply with, rely on, or evangelize any one set of religious principles. There are many people who are hospitalized and in need of someone to listen to all their fears, pains, and the deep needs of their souls. Their recovery program required that they at least remain open to acknowledging a higher power greater than themselves to support them in their quest for sobriety.

They sometimes wanted to talk to a pastor of their religious preference, and yet many simply longed for a listening and compassionate ear, perhaps a prayer or a blessing upon request.

ACT TWENTY-THREE. SAINTS/SINNERS?

The first patient assigned to my counsel at the treatment center was a young black woman I will call Rochelle. I went to meet her in the detoxification unit and she screamed at me: "Get the hell outta here, you fucking white religious freak!" Terrified, I split. My supervisor was sympathetic but would not change the patient assignment. I would be Rochelle's counselor for four weeks. Four! I needed a "higher power" more than she did!

I wondered if there was a trigger, other than the pangs of detoxification, for Rochelle's hostile outburst. She had probably reacted to the little cross I wore. It was a gift to me from my second husband and I still treasure it, because it has an empty space where a crucified corpus would be. That said a lot to me about God's desire to free us from suffering and pain, not impose it. We did enough of that all by ourselves. I resolved not to wear that cross while I worked at this treatment center. My resolve failed.

I wallowed in the Serenity Prayer, the prayer recovering people often use at their meetings.

> *God, grant me the serenity to accept the things I cannot change,*
> *the courage to change the things I can,*
> *and the wisdom to know the difference.* AMEN

While I focused on the serenity to accept what I couldn't change, that is, Rochelle's animosity toward me. I *could* stop wearing my cross. I *could* make myself look completely neutral and safe. I could. But I didn't.

When Rochelle was discharged from the detox unit and released into the continuing program of education and counseling support to help her sustain sobriety, she came to my office. I had my cross on. Rochelle poured out her story to me and I listened with compassion. Just as she was getting ready to leave the session, she pointed to my cross. "Oh, that is such a beautiful little cross, so small, and is it empty?" "Would you like to see it close up?" I offered. She nodded. I removed the cross and handed it to her. She held it and fingered it briefly. I resisted a tiny temptation to give it to her, thank God. She returned it to me with a big grin and a thanks. I did not resist the temptation to consider myself a hot shot chaplain, but I did remember to fondle my small cross and thank Jesus for his corpuscular "absence" from this cross.

ACT TWENTY-FOUR. TRUSTWORTHY SPIRITUALITY

My trustworthy guideposts of faith had always been Scripture, prayer, AND the God within me whose immanent holiness grounded me *and* let me simultaneously follow the stretching and wandering of my heart with the guidance of the Holy Spirit, already a trained Spiritual Director. I grew to understand my "racismS" as intersectional—layered, real, and multiple.

Sexism, heterosexism, ableism, classism, feminism, socialism, fundamentalism, materialism, intellectualism, consumerism—and of course racism. An unmanageable overwhelming pile. Life without all these -isms is free—and possibly impossible.

SCENE SIXTY-FIVE. PRAYERS IN THE BIBLE

I am my prayer to you, prayed the psalmist in Psalm 109 (P. Greenberg translation).

How does one become one's own prayer? It is not by working obsessively, seeking answers to your prayers. That is what I came to call teeth-grinding idiocy! It is rather by slowing down enough to uncross your eyes, see beyond your own desires, slide off the throne of your ruling desires, let go of your immediate worry, release your held breath, open your clenched fists, and allow your willing tears to flow freely. This is how to give the Divine Spirit stretching space in your soul, and how to cleanse yourself of racismS. I discovered this practice when I went on silent retreats in which prayer was about the only bloody thing I did, besides keeping my daily appointments with a spiritual director. Other than that I was swathed in silence even at meals. I got to know my soul.

Sometimes, the little bird in PD Eastman's children's book *Are You My Mother?* popped into my mind. Finally, exhausted with all his questions and quests, he knelt on his tiny exhausted wee bird legs and became a prayer.

SCENE SIXTY-SIX. A PRAYER ROSE

On retreat at night in the darkened chapel at Mercy Center in Madison, Connecticut, I knelt alone and gazed at the elongated oil portrait of a single rose by Mary Daly, RSM. The enormous rose had a long stem, thorns, and bursting petals against the background of a faintly visible green cross. The portrait hung behind the tabernacle. It looked like the sacred heart of Christ, not bloodied or dead, but beckoning, thorns and all.

I wanted to walk into this rose. The tabernacle below the rose contained the sacrament consecrated as Christ's body and blood. It was locked. I was locked out. I knew where the key to that tabernacle was. I debated a break-in. The next day I unlocked the tabernacle, popped one wafer into my mouth, left the door ajar for a brief moment, then closed it and returned the key to its rightful place. I glanced about. There were no tabernacle cops in sight. There is nothing more fun than holy mischief.

ACT TWENTY-FOUR. TRUSTWORTHY SPIRITUALITY

SCENE SIXTY-SEVEN. BREAKING UP THE OLD BOYS' CLUB

In 1974, and again in 1975, groups of Episcopal women deacons, inspired by their call to priesthood, got political. *They organized to lobby for full inclusion. Some willing retired bishops broke ranks to ordain them outside of canonical regulations. Prayer, communicating with one another, discovering shared desires led these women to disobedience—and success, not triumph.*

These women, on whose shoulders I stood as I'd pursued my own call to priesthood in the Episcopal Church, acted together to break the law, a small but not insignificant sound barrier in patriarchal Episcopal Church politics. It would take a long time for the institutional Church to swallow the law whole, to unlock its ancient heart, and in time ordain women as priests—and eventually as bishops. I learned how to wait without patience, to get support and never to give up.

SCENE SIXTY-EIGHT. THE SYROPHOENICIAN (CANAANITE) WOMAN

Biblical characters, to me, were not without flesh. There was always their story. The woman in this small story counted almost as much to me as contemporary women who had paved the way to ordination for us all. It had taken me eleven years (usually four) of building political awareness, shaping up my own soul, and prayer-begging to be ordained priest.

I identified with this Syrophoenician woman, because she too was an outsider/foreigner, a noisy threat, a Greek, a Gentile, "banging on doors," annoying the Rabbi, the Teacher who was on a mission to secure the promised land for his people the Jews. She disrupted the ordered cultural/religious politics of the day as she pursued Jesus, who had his own politics. Her daughter was near death. She begged and bothered Jesus who turned her away *three* times (Matthew 15:21-28). "I came for my people Israel!" he told her. She pushed: "It's not fair to take the children's bread and throw it to the dogs." (Mark 7) Jesus, probably feeling bullied, replied: *"Let the children be fed first, for it is not fair to take the children's food and throw it to the dogs."* Ouch! This heroic woman spoke back , saying: *"Sir, even the dogs (non-Jews) under the table eat the children's crumbs."*

The woman went home and found her daughter healed.

From her story I always get a blast of spiritual courage. Okay, kudos for Jesus too.

SCENE SIXTY-NINE. DEEPER PAIN. DEEPER PRAYER

Years later in 2002 I felt just like this Syrophoenician woman when my beloved youngest son John lay near death in the Intensive Care Unit at Bridgeport Hospital. He had suffered through several surgeries for ulcerative colitis. There was promise for repair and construction of an ersatz colon, but the post-surgical remaining intestinal track had adhered—entirely stuck together, impassable. The surgeon operated again to cut all the folds apart one from another, restitched each separately, refolded the lot, closed up, then told us he hoped it would hold well enough to enable digestion. Would my thirty-two year old son ever eat or drink anything by mouth again? Would he live? The surgeon was honest enough to say he hoped so. I prayed without ceasing and put my heart into the care of that Syrophoenician mother whose exquisite self-humbling, not to mention her poke at religious exclusivity, gave me hope.

My prayers, along with those of colleagues, parishioners, family, and monastic communities, were as intense and ceaseless as those of that Syrophoenician woman.

ACT TWENTY-FOUR. TRUSTWORTHY SPIRITUALITY

With John's permission I share one astonishing healing moment. The hospital chaplain who was Jewish and I stood on either side of John's bed. We decided to say together a prayer we both knew by heart: Psalm 23. John later shared his own experience at that moment, a moment when he was at the point of giving up. He said his whole room suddenly filled with a very bright light. It lasted just seconds. "I suddenly decided to live. I wanted to live. I really wanted to live."

We still laugh about times John came to visit us at St. John's parish in Gloucester, MA. where Dick was Rector and where I had been the Priest Associate, since 1997. John went to church with us. "Mom, how come so many people here know me? They say hello to me by name, as if they knew me?"

Prayer is deep, wide, mysterious, and inexplicably far-reaching.

ACT TWENTY-FIVE. MOVING

When Jesus healed the blind beggar, Bartimaeus, he first inquired: "What would you like me to do for you?" Such a dumb question. Wasn't it obvious? Yes, of course. In Bartimaeus's story, however, Jesus simply told him, without messianic bragging, that he was healed. No messianISM here.

SCENE SEVENTY. GLOUCESTER-ISM?

Dick and I had moved from Connecticut to Gloucester, Massachusetts, in 1997. We had experienced plenty of unsatisfactory, even unpleasant, interviews in Connecticut. We hated to leave our children and theirs behind, *and* we wanted to stand together as priests of Word and Sacrament so we turned to seek a new experience, a new state that had no biases about our divorce/remarriage status—and my poor little battered gender.

Expectations can be hilarious.

We arrived after a sad, teary, and strenuous move, as most moves are. We drove over the bridge into Gloucester on a fog-bound, cold and dreary February day. We had booked a motel for one night, because the moving van would not arrive at the parish rectory until the next day. Where would we find a restaurant for dinner? All

ACT TWENTY-FIVE. MOVING

we really needed at this point was wine anyway. The motel owner gave us a few ideas, recommending Schooners, on the road that runs along the harbor. The owners were friendly and welcoming, and I never—ever before or since—tasted shrimp cocktail like this one. The owner told us that his recipe for cooking freshly caught shrimp was "a secret"—apparently his alone. Schooners, although it changed names a few times in the ten years we lived in Gloucester, became our restaurant of choice on most Sunday evenings. It took time to grieve and adjust.

* * * *

Gloucester is a beautiful island and not *really* an island. The bridge extends like an ongoing road off route 128 highway into a rotary—often all befogged. Mystical! Brigadoon-ish.

* * * *

Dick, whose heritage is Italian, Neapolitan, was excited that this new location would be spectacularly Italian—full of great pasta, wonderful sea waters, beaches, and liberal Democrats. Well, the sea-beaches and the pasta were abundant, but the politics was distinctly mixed and local/eccentric—uniquely Sicilian. Gloucester itself was not *really* an island. Or was it? Jokes abounded about people never "crossing the bridge"—going off island. Gloucester is like a fishing clique, living under the threat of impending legal restrictions on overfishing, thus endangering their livelihood, their identity.

We discovered quickly that if you weren't from Gloucester you were, well, not from Gloucester, not a Glawsta girl or guy. How naive we were to imagine that this parish would be different, more hospitable. I mean, we did know what an Episcopal church was. That, it turned out, was about all we knew.

Dick's first sermon articulated two versions of Christianity—one he thought true to the gospel of Christ and the other not. The next week he preached about a story from the Old Testament. After church I overheard an angry young man comment to another parishioner: "Is he even *allowed* to preach from the OLD Testament?" Someone else said: "What about HER?" A man looked down on me one Sunday and, with a challenging tone, asked: "Do you believe Jesus was divine?" I looked up at him. "Of course. You don't think I'd be praying all these prayers to just any old guy, do you?"

Much of this whispery talk was underground, but gossip seeped out. An elderly parishioner, herself not a native Gloucesterian, adopted us and invited us for sumptuous dinners. I felt hopeful. None of this was anyone's fault. It was about this culture, differences, assumptions, and enough grit to make choices—not from right/wrong or good/bad dualistic stances, but from what we all called divine Grace, lavishly sprinkled with humor.

The first Easter that I preached I opened with my best Boston accent: "It's Eastah in Glostah!" Everyone laughed together.

I prayed for us and for the parish. God was good enough and big enough to listen without judgment. Dick stayed steady and got to know people, as did I. He opened his door to any and all parishioners. I learned that Jesus must obviously have been Sicilian. I mean look how much time he spent on beaches dining on fish!

I joined a Coalition to Prevent Domestic Abuse. We raised awareness. A local female artist designed a bronze statue of a woman with her young child, clinging to her skirts, looking out to sea. She was lonely, longingly praying for her fisherman spouse to be safe and come home. Slowly we felt at home.

We met a black man who loved the liturgy of the Mass, but brought his own "jesus," wafers consecrated by a pastor in his

ACT TWENTY-FIVE. MOVING

own cultural tradition. He came to the altar anyway, and we always gave him a smile and a blessing.

We welcomed a black woman who had fled from an island where there was chaos, fear and oppression. A generous parishioner helped her emigrate and send her sons to school and college in this USA.

An old salt Gloucesterian argued with me regularly that women could not be priests. She was adamant, trained in theology at a conservative Christian university and took every word of holy writ literally. Yet we liked each other. One day she sat me down, patted my knee and told me that she had poured over Scripture and found an old woman named Anna who hung out in the temple, praying every day, and actually bore witness to the child Jesus as the savior when his parents brought him to be presented at the Temple. Anna was a prophet! Conclusion: "If an old woman like that could speak in Church, other women could too" I was in.

It was increasingly obvious to me that racial prejudice, favored whites for no reason whatsoever! Institutionalized religion was STUCK in history, systemic patriarchy, ignorance, fear, misuse of biblical texts, and downright stupidity.

Gloucester began to breathe into its own unique holiness. We led and followed and spent just over ten amazing years there where we grew to know and love many good people.

SCENE SEVENTY-ONE. BACK TO A CITY

Having grown up in big cities (New York and Harrisburg) Dick and I both carried a certain irrational longing to live in a city once more. But where? Boston seemed quite unmanageable, and also expensive and full of neighborhood racial separations.

What about Cambridge? In 2007, a clever realtor told us there were some properties in North Cambridge that *might* be affordable. We found one such place, received some financial assistance from family, and bought a condo/townhouse with four floors and a working basement filled with floor to ceiling bookshelves!

We lived near Danehy Park where people of many cultures, colors, and religious traditions walked, played sports, and jogged together regularly. AND, Gran Gusto within easy walking distance became our favorite Italian restaurant.

Living in this townhouse was like living in a vertically stretched accordion. Contrary to the customary way of staging real estate property as if it were lived in—as if no buyer had an imagination at all—this townhouse at first showing was empty, save for a solo bowl of apples on the kitchen counter.

Each of us had privacy. The bottom floor was designed with a separate entrance, a small waiting room area including a bathroom, adjoining a larger space in case one of us decided to see private clients. It was also convenient for a visiting granddaughter to sneak out and party while we—innocently naive grandparents—slept two floors up. We shared the living area, kitchen, dining area, and living room. The top floor bedroom was as big as the whole footprint of the condo. Privacy and intimacy were available, a mere staircase in between.

We ran and hollered up and down those stairs.

Resources emerged like pennies from heaven, and we bought this ingenious, free standing condo, clustered into a small complex with one house and six other units.

* * * *

ACT TWENTY-FIVE. MOVING

People of all colors and languages wearing various garb, celebrated holidays. Of course I knew we were near Harvard and Boston where urban cultures and neighborhoods thrived, and of course I knew that all this was exceptional, privileged, and unique. Still, riding the T (MTA, the Metropolitan Transit Authority)—subway—was a joy except at rush hours. Remember "Charlie on the MTA" who rode back and forth all day and night, according to the 1949 campaign song? We enjoyed easy access to Boston. Even the subway crowd itself was technicolored and delightful, especially after I got over my horror at being offered a seat by a young person. I proudly declined. Soon, I accepted. Yes, I was an aging woman.

We loved ethnic restaurants, tried all kinds of foods, and even found an Episcopal Church in Charlestown, just north of Boston where we volunteered to become Priests Associate. Their parish matriarch was adamant that women should NOT be priests. I didn't argue. With time she admitted tacitly that I *might* be okay and invited me to deliver the memorial homily after her son died. She never understood why she got older and older and God took her son. Thank heavens I did NOT defend God, but simply listened to her grief. Freedom of thought matters.

Our neighborhood, was, I imagined, exactly how God created the world to be.

Only once did I feel a twinge of racism. One evening when I was walking home from the subway stop at dusk, I decided to take a turn in the park. Full darkness descended quickly. Everything turned black. No one else was around. I quickened my pace—too old to run of course. My fear was racist!

SCENE SEVENTY-TWO. WRITING MY MEMOIR

In retirement I began to write my own "once upon a time" story. I took a memoir writing class at Curry College and dabbled about, chapter after chapter. I am allergic to chronology, in part because it ties me down, in part because I can't remember dates, and in part because some instances are eternal. Dick, who has mastered chronology would scream dates and times at me whenever I cupped my hands and screamed out: "WHEN? WHERE?"

I wanted to write my personal story. I also wanted to make a case that alarmed me: I simply did NOT believe in gendered theology. I did NOT believe in trying to confine Divinity to masculinity. My editor told me: "Lyn, you need to make a case ! What do you want your reader to learn or know?" The title popped off a tee shirt and onto my book: *God Is Not a Boy's Name; Becoming Woman. Becoming Priest* was published in 2016 by Wipf & Stock. Thank you to the Episcopal Women's Caucus for their good humor and to my publisher who believed in, or wasn't afraid of, my politics.

Now I write to liberate Divinity and myself from death by Whiteout.

ACT TWENTY-SIX. HEALING MENTORS ALONG MY WAY

Finding accompanists to enrich my soul mattered. Mentors are people who know the ropes of struggle, the tossing and turning of joy and strife. They are people who pray and often people who have experienced hurt personally and institutionally, often because they have bucked the institutional system and its rules. These are they who, no matter their individual callings, rose above the temptations of ism-ISM—rigidly attachments to ONE way of thought or life.

* * * *

The Rev. Elmore McKee was an Episcopal priest who had been defrocked, stripped of his professional stature because of his divorce at a time when cleric divorce was condemned by the Church. Such a penalty was harsh and extremely unjust!

In the late 1970's I had been turned down twice in the ordination process in Connecticut. A priest mentor in a neighboring parish suggested I talk with Elmore McKee.

Elmore McKee had no political clout, but he sure was able to give me large doses of heart. I poured my story, my tearful pain, my shame, my sins into his listening ears. In his presence I felt consecrated. I glimpsed his own pain, although he never talked directly about it. He knew what such rejection *felt* like, because he too had divorced and remarried. He occasionally interrupted our sessions to tend to his wife who had dementia. He was remarkably loving and attentive to her presence in the next room. "Are you all right, my darling?" Elmore's deposition was the Church's loss.

He talked so much about the value and wonder of lay ministry that I once asked him whether there was any room for priests in his definition of ministers of the Church. We laughed together. Elmore died in 1988, the year after I was ordained priest. He had been a "priest" to me.

Divorce is rarely without some good reason! The Episcopal Church, in time, relaxed its rigid moral and ecclesial spine.

* * * *

Madeleine L'Engle, author and my spiritual director was impatient with the Church's resistance to women's ordination. She was confident I would be ordained. She was, however, very rigidly opposed to divorce, except in situations where it was inevitable—near-necessary. She told me to talk to women I respected, six of whom were divorced and six of whom had stayed in long-term marriages. She was intent on making sure I understood what a "rough" process divorce could be.

I found enough women, all faithful, divorce or no divorce. Their varied experiences helped me as I prepared once again to attempt ecclesiastical suicide. To summarize my findings: The women who had divorced could *not* imagine themselves growing old and needful with their present spouse. The women who stayed in the marriage *could* see themselves growing old and needful with their present spouses, with whom there was mutual trust.

ACT TWENTY-SIX. HEALING MENTORS ALONG MY WAY

When I moved through the ordination process once again, I heeded Madeleine's own final commandment: "Now my dear," she said in the fullness of her certitude. "When you get ordained, and you will, do *not* become a little man." Yes, ma'am.

* * * *

The Rev. Pierre Wolff, an Episcopal priest and Jesuit, knew more than I'd imagined. He had "divorced" his Roman Catholic Church, principally because of the way they treated and perceived women—institutional sexism.

Pierre gave me his own discernment wisdom—what to say when things feel overwhelming: "*Doucement, cherie.*" Take it easy. I say it all the time to myself.

ACT TWENTY-SEVEN.
SEASONING *ALL* SAINTS

Even after I'd been ordained priest for over ten years, I hardly felt like a pro. I gave parish ministry a try and found it not a fit for my gifts and my need to feel, yes, safe enough to shine, to be free enough to declare wild truths about divine sponsorship of every ounce of life— from the tiny flower pushing and poking up through the pavement of city sidewalks to the final sighing breath of a famished beggar huddled against the cold hug of concrete.

SCENE SEVENTY-THREE. FINDING PARTICULAR PLACES

The clerical-ISM in parish ministry was stifling, not to mention lonely. I trained for pastoral counseling work and, in time, became a Fellow in AAPC (American Association of Pastoral Counselors), and set up my own practice. I also trained as a Spiritual Director and became a member of Spiritual Directors International (SDI). I was proud and grateful too to function as a non-stipendiary Priest Associate at St. John's, Gloucester.

In time I started a monthly Holy Eucharist called *The Spirituality Mass* for recovering addicts on Sunday evenings at St. Alban's parish in Simsbury, thanks to the generosity and support of the

ACT TWENTY-SEVEN. SEASONING ALL SAINTS

rector there. That ministry was a joy to me. It provided a connection between my ministry with recovering addicts and my own membership in AlAnon.

Eventually, I partnered with another counselor, and we established a private practice in pastoral counseling. Our office was tucked neatly and almost anonymously into a small now unused library space below the sanctuary in the neighboring United Church of Christ. There were rumors that we were lesbians, but no one asked us directly. We laid low. On Sundays I served as a non-stipendiary Sunday Priest Associate at St. John's, Gloucester, with regular opportunities to preside at Eucharist and to preach. It was ideal except for missing my children.

I am white. I felt locked out by whites. I became absolutely sure that Divinity was both gender-free *and* race-free. We "racists" had to reckon with our own turf wars.

SCENE SEVENTY-FOUR. DEEPENING RACIAL POTENTIATION

Is anything ever rigidly black and white? No!

Often when clergy gather at the annual clergy conference they want either to gossip among themselves, confront the bishop about some itch, or whine while sitting in the bar for idol chit-chat over martinis. Occasionally . . . . . . serious conversations do happen.

At such a conference in 2019 Massachusetts clergy gathered to listen to the dynamic black woman priest, the Rev. Canon Kelly Brown Douglas, theologian and president of Episcopal Divinity School (EDS) at Union Theological Seminary, New York, and Canon Theologian of Washington National Cathedral. Her lectures— intellectually illuminating and emotionally honest— surpassed her impressive resumé.

What I remembered most vividly was her anguish about her growing son's safety in this country—anywhere. Would he be safe? Would he stay alive? Such questions I have worried about as well, mostly in relation to alcohol abuse. I have felt frightened for a son who nearly died after surgeries, for daughters in difficult marriages, and for another who travels the world on business. But I never had to say: "Will my child be shot?"

* * * *

During the afternoon break, Dick and I decided to engage two black male clergy friends over lunch and through the extended afternoon break time. It felt urgent to us all to get serious and personal about our experiences with racism. We told each other our *personal* experiences of racism including the larger issues of geographical biases, and even another potentially toxic ISM, patriotISM, which when carried too far becomes violent.

I spoke about Carol Lee and the racist decision I had once made that left a mark on my own racial conscience. I also spoke about gender bias and patriarchy.

Dick spoke about a black family whose hospitality to him during his college years was extraordinary, yet when the time came for graduation and celebratory dinners, he knew his own white family would not understand his desire to invite a black family to his celebratory dinner. How grateful he remains for the black family's gracious understanding.

One male colleague shared how hard it was to be brown, thanks to mixed parentage, and how difficult it was to be able to "pass" for *either* color. I thought that would be ideal. Not so. Even now, I think how foolishly inaccurate the word "pass" could be. We use it to refer to biological death. There's no going back. Carol Lee couldn't "pass" for white, nor I for black. This mixed-race man

ACT TWENTY-SEVEN. SEASONING ALL SAINTS

used the word "passed" to speak of his skin color. He was black but could "pass" for white.

The other colleague spoke about what it meant to be definitely dark black and originally from another country where color consciousness was a different issue: Black was dominant and normal and white was odd.

Our deep conversations over time were fruitful for us all, and we stayed lunch buddies for some time. Our conversations were filled with honesty, wit and soul.

* * * *

I was invited to preach at St. Cyprian's Episcopal Church in Boston. It was both shocking and thrilling to look out at a sea of black faces. I focused on the Gospel's awareness of justice for all peoples and spoke directly to the immediate concern about racial and gender injustice at the polls. My sermon was punctuated by "say it, sister" and "amen" from congregants. When I concluded, the whole congregation burst into applause. I asked the Deacon: "Do they always do this?" He shook his head from side to side and grinned.

I think I flew all the way home with sure and certain knowledge that the Episcopal liturgy, could be a ritual sturdy enough for *all* races to worship together.

SCENE SEVENTY-FIVE. BLESSING ALL SAINTS

Whenever I presided at the Eucharist where all children were welcomed, they knelt with bowed heads for a blessing, I touched each child's head gently and used a paraphrase of ancient biblical words to offer each one a blessing at the altar rail.

> May God bless you and keep you
> May the face of God shine upon you
> > —and from within you—
> This day and always. (*Numbers 6:24, YHWH to Moses, paraphrased*)
> AMEN.

Some children were obedient to their parents' wishes that they not receive Holy Communion until they were confirmed. Children find ways. One Sunday a very small saint, stood and white-knuckled the altar rail so as not to topple over backwards. She tilted her head up to give me a broad grin and a giggle. I grinned back as I blessed her forehead. I felt equally blessed.

ACT TWENTY-EIGHT. HOLINESS OF WORD AND SACRAMENT. WHOSE?

I do not believe that Holy Scripture should be taken literally. There must be room between the lines for creative spiritual imagination, interpretation, and ongoing scholarly research—not to mention Mystery. I respect the cosmic breadth of Divinity.

Holiness is a moveable feast. To be holy is to be earthly *and* heavenly at once. Your unfolding story is the scripture of your life.

SCENE SEVENTY-SIX. SCRIPTURES

Every Sunday in many Christian churches, the lector ends the biblical reading saying *The Word of God* or *The Lord*. Whose Lord? Oh, Lord, am I just too picky?

Small stories of deep meaning come to each one of us, in all religions and through all spiritualities, ancient and modern. From such inaudibly audible communications come stories, both tender and fierce—all mobilized by Love. The Bible is Holy Word, according to whose Lord?

SCENE SEVENTY-SEVEN. EVERY STORY NEEDS A RITUAL PRACTICE.

When I read the small book *I and Thou,* by Polish-American Rabbi Abraham Joshua Heschel, I knew I'd found the heart of my own and my late Jewish grandfather's spirituality. Both Heschel's spirituality and his social justice activism grew from prayer **within** this intimate God's presence. There was no separation between Heschel's religious faith, his rituals, his stories, and his politics. To me, Heschel became a spiritual giant, even though he was a very short man.

In 1968, Rabbi Heschel was engaged in protest marches and demonstrations against the Vietnam War. One Sabbath his brother

ACT TWENTY-EIGHT. HOLINESS OF WORD AND SACRAMENT. WHOSE?

protesters and friends, the Rev. William Sloane Coffin and the Rev. Dr. Martin Luther King, Jr., came to Heschel's apartment and were greeted with this welcoming exuberance: "You are just in time for the last bit of disengagement from the world we have to change . . . Shabbat!" Heschel let Coffin hold the ritual spices and King the candle while they chanted the prayers, smelling the spice box and collectively drinking a sip of wine. Then Heschel told Coffin and King the story of the wise men of Chelm who deliberated over whether people grew from the feet up or from the head down. The answer was neither. Quoting the *va-yetel el echav*, he said that individuals grow from within and eventually move beyond their own egos towards other people. "Here's to the world's outgrowth of selfishness towards the humanities . . . "L'Hayim!"

The Rev. Daniel Berrigan a Roman Catholic priest, called Heschel's practice of uniting prayers and social action for justice "an ecumenism I could take seriously." (p.195 *Abraham Joshua Heschel. A Life of Radical Amazement,* biography by Julian Zelizer, 2021)

Holiness belongs to everyone everywhere always. It grows from within. It is the star of your own story. You'll recognize it. You'll remember it. You'll outgrow your own ego. You'll find your words and your rituals. You'll pass it on—over and over.

Mine is ours. I is we. They are us.

SCENE SEVENTY-EIGHT. DAILY LIFE SACRAMENTALITY

Is the parish budget a sacrament—an outer sign of an inward grace? Money is the outer sign of the inner grace of generosity. So why is there usually such a furor, such argumentation when it comes to preparing a budget? All kinds of clever names have been devised to disguise the idolatrous practice known as wallet-worship.

What if we spoke of pledging/giving money as a *sacramental* act, rather than a *sacrificial* act? We might unclench our fists and allow God into our sacred wallets.

We might understand that most racismS are based in cultural practices not divine dictates. Using metaphors to connect daily life with sacramental acts helps.

* * * *

Baptism is like the first bath. The outer grace is that this babe gets an official certificate of membership. The deeper grace is the delight a whole community feels at a Baptism. They show up in droves. They make a joyful noise. The infant won't remember it, but this is her or his or their first standing ovation.

I once witnessed an adult baptism. It was thrillingly different. This aging woman had attended church, feeling uncertain of many things including herself. She participated regularly in the community and received Holy Eucharist, even though she was not yet baptized—the wrong order, according to the rules. Order does not a Christian make, does it?

Holy Communion/Eucharist is food to nurture and sustain life all along the way. Eucharist is a meal that feeds us body and soul.

Ordination creates order. When I was ordained priest on March 25, 1988, I felt such internal disorder, such paranoia, that, after all this struggle, it might not happen—or worse, that I'd faint under the weight of a bunch of priests with their pile of hands on my one small head as the Bishop of Connecticut, suffering from a head-cold of some magnitude, pronounced the sentence that would make me a priest.

What to my wondering eyes should appear as I looked at the photos? My pastoral counseling supervisor was in the circle of

ACT TWENTY-EIGHT. HOLINESS OF WORD AND SACRAMENT. WHOSE?

Episcopal priests laying hands onto my head at that moment of my ordination. Only Episcopal clergy are authorized to ordain. I never laughed so hard in my life. Then I panicked. Would this "illegal" presence invalidate the ordination? The "illegal" presence of one set of hands would probably never be spotted. It never was.

In any ordering there is always some disordering. That's what makes ALL of it holy.

SCENE SEVENTY-NINE. LEARNING TO READ THE FLESH

Is the Bible's Word/words itself a sacrament? Does Divinity write on my flesh? If so, on all of it or part of it? I was in danger of turning into a literalist as if every word over centuries was *gospel*. All these words and stories, I realized, are written on my flesh, into my experience. My own flesh felt as fragile as stained glass and yet unbreakable. Do figures jump from the stained glass and into my soul? Did Divinity self-inscribe on our flesh? Mine too? Are we all sacraments, holy in some way—outer signs of inner invisible graces?

Here's a story. It happened in my office at the Alcohol/Drug Rehabilitation where I worked. A young man came to see me. The staff often sent hard spiritual cases to me, as if I had a corner on the marker of Higher Power. com. The young man slouched into a chair and folded his arms, body language for NOT ME. he had never heard of God. Frankly, I had never heard of anyone who had never heard of God. Honestly, he was more honest than others who came in announcing that their whole life plan was neatly tied up and boxed.

We sat in a silence that felt as deadly as any one of the seven deadlies. Damn, I thought. Then Help. Then silence. Neither of us moved. Then a thought came to me. *Did you ever find yourself all alone and helpless and go somewhere into a field or a woods and shout HELP?*

Oh yeah, he said. All the time.

Well, who did you think you were calling to?

Oh, he said. Then again, *Oh.* I never saw him again, but he lives on in my heart-prayers.

* * * *

But surely God is Love, right? Yes.

How flimsy, misused, manipulated, overused, and sentimental that word is. Nevertheless, when I say Love I immediately know how vulnerable God is, I am, we all are. *Love, let us note, is always in the present tense.* (Hope and Faith are future-oriented.)

* * * *

In February, 2022, I listened to a recorded conversation between Pope Francis and Loyola University students from north, central and south America. The program was sponsored by Loyola University of Chicago, Institute of Pastoral Studies, and requested by Pope Francis who wanted to know what young adults think and ask. The program was called, "Building Bridges: A Synodal Encounter Between Pope Francis and University Students."

I was fascinated as I watched and listened and took notes, just as the Pope did. He began by defining the word *synod* which means meeting or assembly of clergy. Then he stressed *synodality* as a journey together in which LISTENING would be the basic skill necessary to replace walls—all our "perfect little boxes." We build bridges as we go. That's not easy if you've ever watched a bridge being built.

ACT TWENTY-EIGHT. HOLINESS OF WORD AND SACRAMENT. WHOSE?

One female student mustered the courage to ask Pope Francis directly about God. "How is God?" she asked. I cringed, expecting a lecture about God as superpower. Answer: *"God is close, merciful, tender and compassionate. And that is all you need to know."*

ACT TWENTY-NINE. RETIREMENT?

Does anyone ever retire? No, one might, however, grow backwards with aging. Or one might simply retire earlier to bed and later to rise. Or you pursue a hobby you've always wanted to try out? Or read whatever interests you, and befriend anyone you want to anywhere? Some of us grieve and some pretend to be just fine. Still others feel lost or embittered.

You see, there is NO RIGHT OR WRONG WAY and only ONE CERTAIN FACT: you are aging, and one day you will die. May I recommend reading the comics more closely than what passes for "news"—then laugh yourself to death, one day a certainty for us all no matter what. (My favorite street beggar in Boston laughed all the time. He got more money!) There's always a story!

SCENE EIGHTY. KEEPING ON KEEPING ON

I am in my lazy eighties. I never set the alarm clock. I wake up to birds. I love celebrating the Eucharist—Word and Sacrament—with just the two of us. We alternate the role of presider. We sing and read Scriptures in aging voices. We preach to, or at, each other, using the latest translations of psalms and hymns.

ACT TWENTY-NINE. RETIREMENT?

I am especially fond of *The Inclusive Bible. The First Egalitarian Edition,* sponsored by the Quixote Center, and published in 2007 by Priests for Equality.

Back in 1975, just when I was drawn to follow my own stirred heart, this summary below from *Liturgy for All People* was written as part of the attempt of some post-Vatican II Roman Catholic clergy to examine theological language:

> Sticks and stones may break my bones, but names will never hurt me" says the old proverb. We know now that this is a lie. Words can wound, alienate and degrade people. Language can also affirm and express love. Care for language is a show of concern for people and a revelation of the attitudes of the speaker. . . . Church language is predominantly masculine. Male terms, images, and stereotypes, so-called sexist language, dominate church expression. Such usage is no longer adequate. It is time to build gender equality into the very fabric of church life. The effort to build new gender-balanced ways of speaking helps us toward gender equality for women and men. (from the Preface to *The Inclusive Bible, First Egalitarian Translation*, published in 2007 by Priests for Equality)

How many times the Holy Bible itself has been translated, each time imperfectly!

Chasing Divinity is always playing catch-up.

SCENE EIGHTY-ONE. TOPOGRAPHY?

Don't look up and above for God all the time, look down and all around. I'm not writing about the merits of being a deep sea diver over those of being an astronaut. I'm writing about seeking God within the *depths* of your own flesh and that of others. Be a map!

Kids delight in making mud pies, getting all dirty, slopping the mud all over their small bodies, while giggling with joy at the mess— just as good an image of spiritual joy as something high and mighty and above it all, like heavenward arias or the raised hands of a priest whose face and action you cannot see because his or her back is turned away from you. Don't let God be aloof or arid or disembodied.

SCENE EIGHTY-TWO. CAGED BIRDS?

I actually had *seen* Maya Angelou in person live in Hartford, Connecticut in the late 1980s when she performed at the YWCA in Hartford. Tall and elegant, dressed in elaborate colors and a turban, she strode onto the stage singing in a low-pitched resonant voice. Singing! She seized the large audience's attention immediately. Who dares to be such a commanding presence? Maya Angelou.

This "caged bird" I'd read about in her 1969 book, *I Know Why The Caged Bird Sings.*

In retirement now I watch the scoop and sweep of living birds. Back in the seventies, I too had felt restless and ready to fly—not away from anyone, but rather *towards* my own inner urging to be

ACT TWENTY-NINE. RETIREMENT?

a woman—not confined by traditional "cages" or stereotypes of domesticity. I wanted to fly and plunge.

Angelou's first memoir in her series is a coming-of-age story that "illustrates how strength of character and a love of literature help *overcome* racism and trauma." She is right! Just like divine respect for genetics like blue eyes. Also, God don't make no cages!

Black author, "Toni" Morrison, in her own goodbye and thank you in *The New York Times*, wrote that black author James Baldwin gave her three gifts: "a language to dwell in, a gift so perfect" that it seemed her own; "the courage to live life in and from its belly as well as beyond its edges; and his tenderness and vulnerability, and a love that made one want to be worthy, generous, and strong."

In the 1970s, I was living life from my belly—in my flesh as a mom. Harlem was about to light up with riotous racial strife, but it felt distant to me in my whited-out condition. However, Morrison's stories and her lavish use of words captured my own love of words, and brought me close to Divinity grounded in all flesh NOT to alter it but to LOVE it as it is. (NO, I don't mean avoid doctors or become an anti-vaxer!)

Divinity enlivens the brilliant blooming of potentiation—freely and forever.

SCENE EIGHTY-THREE. "WE FLESH...

Like Toni Morrison, I pursued my everlasting love of words. WORDS had attracted me from early childhood. Imagine loving spelling! Today I write to enliven my connection to Life itself. Words are my icons, why I majored in languages, and why I love *all* stories, as long as wordiness does not blur potency.

In retirement from active ministry, as if there were such a thing as inactive ministry, I read Morrison's 1970 novel, *The Bluest Eye*.

I had never thought about eye color but I realized I'd never seen a black person with blue eyes. My eyes are hazel. I wondered enviously about having blue eyes myself, but then I figured I'd have to have blonde hair to match and thus turn into a trite stereotype. I wanted to be taken seriously just as I am.

Beloved is about a runaway slave who murdered her daughter rather than allowing her to be enslaved. It chilled me to the bone. It stung me with the memory of Carol Lee and my first racist decision. It caused me to wonder if God called Father according to patriarchal culture had murdered Jesus, and it jolted me into realizing that my parents' decision to move to the white suburbs, away from my beloved city was *not*, as my adolescent ego had imagined, to ruin my life. It was White flight.

* * *

It was Morrison's language itself that healed my horrors, taught me to appreciate my own female flesh and fall more deeply in love with the religious idea of Incarnation. This is why *Flesh* appeared suddenly to me as a verb in this passage she wrote about her race.

"In this here place, we flesh; flesh that weeps, laughs; flesh that dances on bare feet in grass. Love it. Love it hard. Yonder they do not love your flesh. They despise it. They don't love your eyes; they'd just as soon pick em out. No more do they love the skin on your back. Yonder they flay it. And O my people they do not love your hands. Those they only use, tie, bind, chop off and leave empty. Love your hands! Love them. Raise them up and kiss them. Touch others with them, pat them together, stroke them on your face 'cause they don't love that either. You got to love it, you! And no, they ain't in love with your mouth. Yonder, out there, they will see it broken and break it again. What you say out of it they will not heed. What you scream from it they do not hear. What you put into it to nourish your body they will snatch away and give you leavins instead. No, they don't love your mouth. You got to love it. This is flesh I'm talking about

ACT TWENTY-NINE. RETIREMENT?

here. *Flesh that needs to be loved. Feet that need to rest and to dance; backs that need support; shoulders that need arms, strong arms I'm telling you. And O my people, out yonder, hear me, they do not love your neck unnoosed and straight. So love your neck; put a hand on it, grace it, stroke it and hold it up. and all your inside parts that they'd just as soon slop for hogs, you got to love them. The dark, dark liver—love it, love it and the beat and beating heart, love that too. More than eyes or feet. More than lungs that have yet to draw free air. More than your life-holding womb and your life-giving private parts, hear me now, love your heart. For this is the prize."*

Godde, help me to *flesh* myself in your mirror, and to love every bit of my own flesh, including my curious supple mind, lodged in my brain and in my heart.

I cannot resist a portion of Angelou's poem on her aging, written as if aging did not exist. I am aging now and I can still breathe in and out—not voluminously but faithfully. Here is a portion of her poem on aging.

> ON AGING by Maya Angelou
>
> When you see me walking, stumbling,
> Don't study and get it wrong.
> 'Cause tired don't mean lazy
> And every goodbye ain't gone.
> I'm the same person I was back then,
> A little less hair, a little less chin,
> A lot less lungs and much less wind.
> But ain't I lucky I can still breathe in.

SCENE EIGHTY-FOUR. RECITATIF

Recitatif is a term I learned when I studied classical music in college. There I discovered a whole new world of beauty without reason. I admit I loved being able to analyze a musical composition and to break it down into movements, themes, styles. I excelled in this analytical part. I learned to love the sounds of each instruments on its own merits, and my ear learned to identify each one. BUT when the professor played a piece cold and asked us to identify the composer, I blanked. Suddenly everything sounded like Beethoven!

Soon, however, I learned to identify the "soul" of a piece!

Toni Morrison wrote many wonderful heart-piercing books, and also a small story called *Recitatif*, published in 1983. It is about two girls, one black and one white. They both grew up in the same orphanage and formed a close-knit and lifelong friendship. A University of Hartford professor I heard speak about this small book called it "only an exercise, not literature." Really?

This piece is/was a *literary* exercise. It depended on how well the author orchestrated words to engage our senses, thus making the theme come alive, to convey the pathological beat of racism, based *entirely* on readers' learned assumptions.

Morrison writes in such a way that it is impossible to tell which girl is white and which is black. I read it, and even though I knew this was the project's goal, I could NOT tell the difference between these two girls/women from any racial perspective at all. NONE—and believe me, I tried.

Morrison successfully portrayed her vision of liberation: "the recognition of somebody in everybody." She resisted categories that are restrictive, assumptive, limiting, and frankly boring—yes, even patriotism, feminism, sexism, and agism.

* * *

ACT TWENTY-NINE. RETIREMENT?

I had not known and liked Carol Lee just because she was black. I knew/liked her through her personality and her emotions, the same way she knew me. Emotional intelligence, the flow of shared feelings, fuels and sustains all relationships. Even deaf people can communicate with wordless touch. Remember Helen Keller's joy at feeling with her hands and lips the sensation of running water when her beloved teacher signed the word W-A-T-E-R onto her hands as she ran water over them. Is not gentle touch a language? The best communicator of wordless love is touch.

Morrison, driven by her expansive vision, wrote an emotion-**free** story into which we could project our own feelings to make the whole come alive. I, for example, remember my own best friends with whom I still connect in spite of geographic separations, even death. I still scan obituaries, briefly grieve, then remember. The process is like the pasted paper chains small kids make in kindergarten—potentially everlasting.

SCENE EIGHTY-FIVE. PERSONAL EMOTIONAL INTELLIGENCE

My feelings all but vanished along with my body after I was sexually molested by an old man who took the empty seat next to me in a New York City theater. I was eight. As his hand ran up my leg, I was paralyzed, save for my left hand that moved to take his hand away—over and over. Later, I felt swathed in shame as if the whole event were my fault. My mind took over and helped me continue to function. Internally I blushed, envisioning myself as a small head with legs.

It took time and therapy to connect with my body's feelings. Anger was the hardest. Anger is also the most "racialized" emotion—those *angry* blacks, those *angry* immigrants, those *angry* cops, those *angry* politicians, those *angry* women and feminists, those *angry* LGBTQs, and those *angry* white supremacists.

YOU DON'T FIGHT FOR PEACE YOU JUST BECOME IT.

Anger, however, is tempting fuel. It taught me to stand up *for* myself not *against* others, as if everything were a battle. Here's a story.

My Crockpot taught me to simmer.

My therapist taught me how to explode safely and before I self-immolated.

I told her I felt restless inside.
She asked if my energy was an animal.
I assessed her as crazy.
She turned away from me and went to her desk.
Stunned, abandoned, and rejected, I pulled out my checkbook to pay for the session.
As I was writing my check, like a good girl, my "bull" arrived —unbidden.

I snorted.
I roared.
I bellowed.
I pawed the rug with my foot.
ROAR.
RAGE.

CALM.
PEACE.

My rage receded, as most storms do. I then felt fully grounded inside myself, and fully sounded out by this therapist who had by now returned to her seat and sat in front of me with a smile—becalmed.

For the very first time—the *very* first time in a couple of years—I noticed that this woman, this therapist, was, yes, beautiful, radiantly so.

ACT THIRTY. LIVING IT ALL TOGETHER?

Aldous Huxley, philosopher and author, once wrote this wisdom: 'Our Kingdom go" is the necessary and unavoidable corollary of 'Thy Kingdom come'...

"Going" is a jerking process! So is "coming" Forgive my unholy language, but you know me by now.

By 2020, racism was headlined all over the world and laid at our national doorstep as a call, I'd say from Divinity, to examine and change our personal and national addiction to racist/sexist/ heterosexist practices, all breeders of destructive rage.

* * * *

The *New York Times Magazine* (7/19/2020) published Isabelle Wilkerson's article "America's Enduring Caste System" in which she imaged caste as the usher's flashlight in a darkened theater silently guiding us to our assigned seats. But who bought the tickets? According to Wilkerson: "The instinctive desire to reject the very idea of current discrimination on the basis of a chemical compound in the skin is an unconscious admission of the absurdity of race as a concept. *With no universally agreed upon definition, we might see racism as a continuum rather than an absolute.*" (Italics mine.)

SCENE EIGHTY-SIX. THE REV. DR. PAULI MURRAY

I read the memoir of Pauli Murray, *Song In a Weary Throat*, published posthumously in 1987 by The Pauli Murray Foundation, and in 2018 by Patricia Bell-Scott, as a Liveright paperback. I read every single word of its 572 pages. Lost in my own struggles to survive patriarchal-ISM, I had missed this "sister" who had lobbied vociferously and against odds on her right to be—to belong—and to become.

* * * *

Pauli was a faithful Bible-aware Christian, orphaned at four yet, in the double entendre ways of Mystery, ended up transferred to the segregated deep south to live with her liberal and unflappable Aunt Pauline who called Pauli "my little boy-girl."

Early on, Pauli felt betrayed by this God who promised a whole kingdom then failed to deliver to the likes of her. She knew that the Lord's Prayer petition, *"Thy will be done"* felt futile. She raged and argued against having to fight for what Christ promised: "It's not fair, Lord!" This showed Pauli's natural courage. She had extraordinary literary, legal, religious, and spiritual intelligence, not to mention herculean persistence and indomitable energy.

It was *not* fair. It *still* is not fair.

To me, the most intriguing small detail of this book is the account of a bus trip Pauli made with a friend. The agony of their experience, being seated on the bus, then being moved, several times, away from their comfortable seats, to the back of the bus. Each time had to pick up all their luggage and belongings and haul it all with them to the rear. The driver didn't care, and sometimes

ACT THIRTY. LIVING IT ALL TOGETHER?

started up the bus AFTER the white travelers were seated up front, but before Pauli and her friend were fully situated. The segregated seating, in quality and quantity, was painfully, bodily, obvious. I cringed reading all this. The process felt "Kafkaesque." Pauli, however, knew she was no cockroach.

She applied her own intelligence, became educated, prayed incessantly for justice and for her personal life and dreams. She received a degree in law and offered her skills to friends. As a faithful Christian woman, she desperately begged God to DO something. After the death of her closest friend Pauli besieged and beseeched God. The prayers of a fiercely loving, committed, and angry woman might have power enough to bend even Divinity. A new thought arrived: *"What if death is a loving mother waiting to enfold us in a protective embrace, rather than the grim reaper I grew up with?"* (p. 553)

And what if gender is too? And what too if the one we call God is DIVINITY, enfolding and informing and repeating itself all the time? I do NOT call God Creator or Mother, even if such terms make more sense. *I call all of it Divinity.*

Pauli later confessed that she was simultaneously praying for herself, because she could not bear to see the suffering of her friend. I too had noticed this double helix of prayer. I prayed my rejecting bishop would drop dead, but all he did was retire, and I got political.

* * * *

Pauli Murray never stopped educating herself, exercising her excellent mind to achieve degrees as an attorney and then in seminary to become the first black woman to be ordained. She rejected the mystical idea of a vocational "call" directly from the Almighty.

So did I. My call was contextual. It began with a tiny book about a God who listened to all "weeny" sounds like the ones God in my childhood book heard. It motivated me to listen, to educate myself, and to turn my anger into fuel. My motives were not pure or bright, but shadowed with personal ambition. Like Pauli, I pursued education and arranged my hours so I would not be that "bad" of a mother. Justifications like that usually wear well—for a time. Like Pauli I pushed on, imagining my clients as sacraments with evocative graces to be discovered, and myself a coal miner in the dark with a searchlight.

SCENE EIGHTY-SEVEN. QUIRKY HISTORY, A MURAL AND A COIN

A lawyer, a priest, and a writer, especially of poems, Pauli Murray was ordained in the little chapel where her grandmother Cornelia had been baptized more than a century earlier as one of "Five Servant Children Belonging to Miss Mary Ruffin Smith." Amazing grace? Also, amazing grit.

I felt a rush of delight at the large mural recently installed in 2002 in the dining hall of Pauli Murray College at Yale, Pauli having been the first black woman to earn her JSD at the Yale law school.

ACT THIRTY. LIVING IT ALL TOGETHER?

Muralist, Mikalene Thomas, '02 said of her creation: "I always knew I wanted something BIG to represent someone whose life did not obey frames: who literally imagined themselves out of Jim Crow North Carolina, out of patriarchy, out of so many limitations that were imposed on them." Head of College, Tina Lu, told the News. "I also wanted a portrait that would always exist in a little bit of tension with the room itself; as Mickalene says, "Pauli in the mural is looking outward."

As much as I admired Pauli Murray for her many achievements and her fame, what I love most is her gift as a poet. She put words together to create beauty *with* deep meaning. Here is a favorite example from *Dark Testament and Other Poems.*

> *Hope is a crushed stalk*
> *Between clenched fingers.*
> *Hope is a bird's wing*
> *Broken by a stone.*
> *Hope is a word in a tuneless ditty—*
> *A word whispered with the wind,*
> *A dream of forty acres and a moment to rest,*

A name and place for one's children
And children's children at last . . .
Hope is a song in a weary throat.

When one can use words in such an artful way, I know that this person truly lived and lived truly—full of grace and grit. I aspired to the same.

* * * *

Amazing addendum: The United States Mint has just issued a 2024 Pauli Murray quarter. The secretary of the Treasury selects from honorees following consultation with the National Women's History Initiative. For more, see *American Women Quarters*.

Heads: George Washington and Liberty on an American quarter.
Tails: The Rev. Dr. Pauli Murray, Episcopal priest, attorney, and poet. Her bespectacled face looks through the O of the word HOPE, "a song in a weary throat."

I am very proud of the 2024 quarter, of the "whiteist" Episcopal Church that ordained Pauli, and of my "racist" country that recognized this black woman on its coinage.

ACT THIRTY-ONE. IDEALLY RETIRED IN WHITESVILLE.

Accepting diversity as a good concept is not the same as living it. There is no sustainable comfort when there is ongoing loss. Everyone pretends, tries to continue doing everything they did before, pushes cheerfulness no matter what (toxic positivity), and tries to ignore the almost daily messages sent from an aging body. We always think those around us will be, and should be, our family. But the fact is that this traditional and static idea is not true. Biological family members often live far away, are too busy with their own lives, or have never had therapy to resolve/heal old wounds. When informed that you are in fact dying, they will show.

Make sure your legal affairs and wishes are in order! (Besides a Will I recommend The Five Wishes, a legal document but with space for more personal information available.)

SCENE EIGHTY-EIGHT. SENIORS PACKING IT IN TOGETHER

Dick and I moved back to Connecticut in 2020 to be closer to most of our children and theirs. Guess what? They *all* had very busy and, gratefully, healthy and creative lives, to manage. They fit us in graciously—all this in the midst of a pandemic, vaccinations, boosters and lockdowns. There would be more to resolve/heal.

The people who offer comfort in this process, besides necessary medical care, are those who live wherever we are.

NEIGHBORS!

But didn't Jesus suggest something like loving our neighbors as ourselves? YES! I never thought I would be living this neighborly wisdom as *literally* as I live it now in this residential retirement community where we moved, knowing no one at all. At least I am a WE, that is, not a single woman aging alone.

Dick and I, now married for thirty-seven years, are grateful for each other. We argue over silly things. Aging is full of losses, often daily of course. Aging is also full of opportunity to make new friends and to reconcile leftover family issues. We laugh most heartily with those who are employed as aides. They are often black and not yet aging in place as we are.

We try to avoid the temptation of allowing differing political views to define friendships. We watch a smattering of news, eat desserts, dine out (including delivered pizza), listen more than talk, sing off key, watch funny movies, even cartoons, and British police dramas from the olden days. We talk with children and grandchildren whenever we can get them to answer their phones. Thank god for mobile phones that text, and for computers that help us ZOOM with old friends—mostly laughing.

Writing enlivens my creativity. I've been working on this new book, keeping my weekly blog brief, and also writing poetry. I read books I WANT to read, and of course I pray without

ACT THIRTY-ONE. IDEALLY RETIRED IN WHITESVILLE.

ceasing, randomly and not in a parish church community, unless the whole Earth is a "church" in which worship is ongoing. We have a community here, and we make the most of our "Whitesville"—the best of it and the worst of it.

EPILOGUE.

One nagging question surfaces every once in a while as I age, and because I obsess Sometimes it comes from one of my four adult children, and sometimes from my naturally inquisitive soul: why—really truly deeply—did my first marriage fail? Did I fail? Did he? Neither. We both simply found someone with whom we shared core values. Love might be a "many-splendored" thing but, trust me, it runs in surges like electricity. Without devotion and strategies for *combat* it withers. Divinity, however, has always been advertised as never-ending Love—unconditional for all creation, all creatures great and small.

* * * *

I remain grateful for the late Rt. Rev. Bishop Barbara Clementine Harris (1930-2020) the first black woman to be consecrated a Bishop in the Episcopal Church in 1989, was a woman of brisk and expansive spirit, and the author of a memoir *Alleluia Anyhow*. After the ceremony a priest bent to kiss her ring, and she said "Forget the ring, sweetie, kiss the bishop." Barbara wrote this blurb for my memoir: *"Brakeman's memoir is a compelling read that carries one along for an intimate ride on her ashes to Alleluia journey. You will careen with her along crooked emotional paths, through turbulent eddies of soul searching, over rough spiritual terrain and out onto*

EPILOGUE.

a broad plain of self healing, health and self worth that continues to stretch before her and many of us."

The Rt. Rev. Barbara C. Harris
Bishop Suffragan, Diocese of Massachusetts (Ret.)

Thank you, Bishop!

* * * *

And I will never forget my own commandment issued by the late author Madeleine L'Engle. I obey this daily: *"Now, my dear, when you get ordained, and you will, do NOT become a little man."* So far so good!

* * * *

Thanks, Mom, for loving me too much. Thanks, Dad, for never letting me win an argument. Thanks, Laurie, for sharing giggles and grief. Thanks, sister writers, for being cheerleaders and critics at once. Thanks, Divinity, for listening to all my weeny sounds. Thanks Jesus, and all Jews, for taking it into the flesh. Thanks, Carol Lee, for not getting lost in a blackout. Thanks, all our children, for patience. Thanks, Dick for loving with occasional impatience. And thanks, Jonathan, for your *sin falta* precision-proofing.